Van Depoele Electric Light Company

Van Depoele Electric Light Company

Manufacture single and multiple current dynamo electric machines,

motors, electric lamps and electro-plating apparatus

Van Depoele Electric Light Company

Van Depoele Electric Light Company
Manufacture single and multiple current dynamo electric machines, motors, electric lamps and electro-plating apparatus

ISBN/EAN: 9783337272487

Printed in Europe, USA, Canada, Australia, Japan

Cover: Foto ©Andreas Hilbeck / pixelio.de

More available books at **www.hansebooks.com**

VAN DEPOELE

ELECTRIC LIGHT COMPAN.

MANUFACTURE

SINGLE AND MULTIPLE CURRENT

DYNAMO ELECTRIC MACHINES,

MOTORS,

ELECTRIC LAMPS,

AND

ELECTRO-PLATING APPARATUS.

———

OWN AND CONTROL THE

VAN DEPOELE PATENTS AND SYSTEM

FOR THE LIGHTING OF

HOTELS, STORES, PUBLIC BUILDINGS, HALLS, FACTORIES, RAILWAY
STATIONS, MINES, TUNNELS, STEAMBOATS, STREETS,
PARKS AND CITIES.

———

GENERAL OFFICES AND WORKS,

203 & 205 VAN BUREN STREET,

CHICAGO, ILL., U. S. A.

--

JUNE 1, 1884.

KNIGHT & LEONARD, PRINTERS,
CHICAGO.

ᴀɴ Depoele Electric Light Company.

Incorporated April 25, 1881.

Paid-up Capital Stock, $1,000,000.

BOARD OF DIRECTORS.

AARON K. STILES,
President Western Fence Company,
Office, 15 to 21 N. Clinton Street, Chicago.

W. H. TURNER.
Turner & Ray, Wholesale Leather and Findings,
Nos. 20 and 22 State Street, Chicago.

FRANK DOUGLAS,
Manfr. of Iron and Wood-Working Machinery,
Nos. 253 and 255 S. Canal Street, Chicago.

E. H. CARMACK,
Ass't Man'r Continental Life Ins. Co., Hartford.
Office, Grannis Block, Chicago.

ALBERT WAHL,
Capitalist, No. 255 Michigan Avenue, Chicago.

CHAS. J. VAN DEPOELE,
Electrician,
Nos. 903 and 905 Van Buren Street, Chicago.

J. W. CALKINS,
President of Thorn Wire Hedge Company,
Chicago.

LOUIS WAHL,
Wahl Brothers, Glue Manufacturers,
Nos. 238 and 240 Randolph Street, Chicago.

CALEB CLAPP,
Clapp & Davies, Wholesale Jewelers,
Nos. 63 and 65 Washington Street, Chicago.

W. A. STILES,
Sec'y and Treas. Thorn Wire Hedge Co.,
Chicago.

JOSEPH A. SLEEPER,
Of Sleeper & Whitton, Attorneys,
Chicago.

OFFICERS AND EXECUTIVE BOARD.

AARON K. STILES, President.

E. H. CARMACK, Treasurer.

THEO. P. BAILEY, Secretary.

CHAS. J. VAN DEPOELE, Electrician.

THOS. S. SPRAGUE (Detroit), Counsel.

FRANKLAND JANNUS (Washington),
Counsel.

JOSEPH A. SLEEPER (Chicago),
Attorney.

TO THE PUBLIC.

–

SINCE issuing our last circular, Electric Lighting has been constantly growing into public favor. The number of Electric Light plants has been steadily increasing, and improvements have been continuously made upon the different systems in use. The Electric Light business has become more generally understood, and people are being educated in electricity, so that they understand it is an element to be used and governed, instead of a mysterious power to be dreaded and shunned.

Electric Light Companies are now formed upon a legitimate and paying basis, and not as stock jobbing companies to fleece the public and enrich the promoters.

The manufacturing of Electric Light machinery and apparatus has become a legitimate business like that of any other machinery.

The Van Depoele Electric Light system has made more progress than any other. Being founded upon a solid basis, after years of trial and experience, there was nothing to be done but to *steadily* advance and perfect the work so ably begun and so thoroughly studied. The Van Depoele Electric Light system does not consist of a dynamo or a lamp, but it embraces a *complete system* of generators and lamps of many kinds, motors and switches and general electric apparatus.

HISTORY OF THE VAN DEPOELE SYSTEM.

MR. VAN DEPOELE is a Belgian, born in 1846. He began the study of electricity when but ten years of age, at the time when the first telegraph lines were established between Poperinghe and Bruges. His father being master mechanic on the railroad at these points, the boy had access to the batteries and other electrical apparatus. He soon constructed batteries, electro-magnets, etc., and with his spare money procured books on natural philosophy and electricity, which were far beyond his class in the college of Poperinghe, where he received his education. In 1861 he produced his first light with a battery of some forty Bunsen cells, which he had to hide from his father's sight, and which could be found to-day between the joists in the garret of the house where they lived. The only ones who witnessed the light were the neighbors and his comrades. The thing leaked out soon, however, and his father chastised him severely for thus spending his time and money in what he called " good for nothing."

The study and experiments, however, continued with increased zeal, he thus passing many a night without sleep. In 1864 the family moved to Lille, France, and in a short time the young man attracted the attention of Dr. Patoir, through his experiments and exhibitions.

The Doctor succeeded in converting the father, who now encouraged him, and allowed him to experiment during his spare time. Young Van Depoele attended regularly the lectures and experiments at the Imperial Lyceum in Lille, from 1864 to 1869, until he came over to this country.

Mr. Van Depoele exhibited his light, and other electrical appliances, in Detroit, Michigan, in 1869, where he acquired subsequently considerable reputation in the manufacture of art furniture. The electrical experiments, however, were not abandoned, but every moment's leisure was spent in the pursuit of his hobby. Several different dynamos and induction machines, etc., were made. His aim all the time was to produce a practical electric light, and he never doubted that he would finally succeed. In 1870 he prepared a battery of one hundred Bunsen's elements, exhibited the light and other experiments to his friends, who remember and bear testimony to his enthusiasm and success. In 1877 a public exhibition was given of his light at Detroit, Michigan, and his friends, after witnessing the results, greatly encouraged him. He built an addition to his shop in which to conduct the experiments, undisturbed by his regular business, which business he turned over to his father.

It was in this shop, and from this time that Van Depoele turned his entire attention to electrical experiments in all directions. Many different styles of lamps were made and experimented with, and not less than fifteen different styles of dynamos were made and tested, with all sorts of combinations and

winding. The division of the current was accomplished, and many more difficult problems solved by these experiments. Most of this machinery and apparatus is to be seen to-day, filling a large room with these curiosities. The studies
and experiments were continued vigorously, and every now and then Van Depoele
gave an exhibition of his light to the public. In 1879 he lighted up Adam
Forepaugh's Circus; a few days later the Detroit Recreation Park, the Detroit
Grand Opera House, etc. These exhibitions attracted the attention of capitalists,
who cheerfully offered their assistance, and the experimenting shops were transferred to the Detroit Novelty Works, in Hamtramck, where several new machines
were built and experiments continued, until in 1880, when a company was formed
to enter upon the manufacture of the electric-light machinery. Finding, however, that Detroit was not the real field, the company was transferred to Chicago,
Illinois, where a new company was formed, being the one in existence to-day.
During all this time Van Depoele has been hard at work to improve his system,
and this by practical experience, and no guess work, until to-day this company
can boast of having the most perfect and simple system in the market.

THE VAN DEPOELE

DYNAMO ELECTRIC MACHINE.

DESCRIPTION OF THE VAN DEPOELE SYSTEM.

THE main features of the Van Depoele dynamo consist in the peculiar disposition of the field magnets, the construction of the armature, the extreme simplicity of all parts of the apparatus (it having fewer parts than any other dynamo made), great compactness, and, above all, the ease of management and control of the current to the work called for. Fig. 1 shows the dynamo with automatic current regulator. The principal parts of the dynamo are:

THE FIELD MAGNETS,

consisting of two large coils of copper wire wound around two soft-iron cores, their north and south poles facing each other, and between these poles revolves the armature. The soft-iron cores of the field magnets are cast on one end to heavy back plates, while to the other end are secured the semi-circular pole pieces between which the armature revolves in close proximity to the latter. The back plates of the magnets are secured between top and bottom plates, holding the whole in position and making a most solid frame. To the lower plate and in its center, which is neutral, are cast two extensions upon which are placed the posts or bearings supporting the armature shaft; this disposition allows the posts to be comparatively short, providing a very rigid support for the revolving armature. Further, the whole frame may be considered as a very long electro-magnet, with its poles inverted toward the center

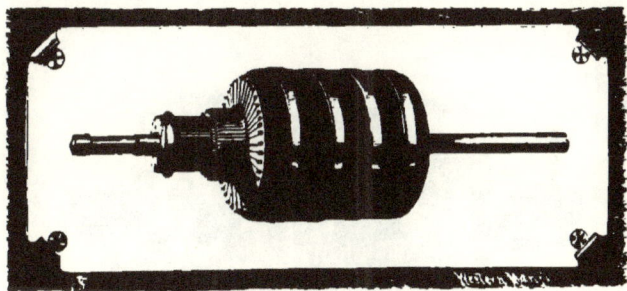

FIG. 2. THE ARMATURE.

THE ARMATURE.

Fig. 2 forms the most important part of the machine, and consists of a frame made of a number of iron bars, each separated from the other; these bars are riveted to the inner and outer periphery of two metal rings, several of these rings being placed between the inner and outer layer of iron bars. And finally, the rings and bars are riveted together so as to form a solid frame. The difference between this form of core and the Pacinotti or Gramme ring will be apparent at a glance: The Gramme ring is composed of several layers of soft-iron wire coiled one upon the other, forming the armature core, upon which the copper wire is ultimately wound in sections; the magnetism of the field can act but very little or not at all upon the copper wire coiled on the inside of the ring thus made, since this wire adds only to the resistance of the machine, without doing any service in the production of useful currents, the only effective portion of the wire being that close to the field and on the outside of the ring; whereas, the Van Depoele armature being built up of several rings — distanced one from the other — and the bars also distanced one from the other, an opening is thus provided all along and around the whole core. It will readily be seen, therefore, that the magnetism of the field can

FIG. 3. THE BRUSH HOLDER.

FIG. 4. END VIEW OF DYNAMO.

easily reach the wire wound on the inside of the cylinder, or armature, making every inch of wire in this armature pass under the direct influence of the *field of force*, thus accounting for the great efficiency of the Van Depoele dynamo.

Another and very important advantage offered by this construction is that these bars being wound (each couple of bars with one section of wire) and the iron bars not touching one another, the magnetization and demagnetization of the same is effected instantaneously, and adds to the efficiency of the machine, since all local action is thus avoided.

It is entirely unnecessary with this armature to provide for ventilation, since there is no heat generated therein, and hence a great saving of power is effected compared with other machines which act as fans, and require considerable power simply to keep up the ventilation.

THE COMMUTATOR

is made up of a large number of copper sections securely held together, and connected to the coils of the armature (see Fig. 2). The brushes and their holders (see Fig. 3) are made substantial, easily handled and adjusted, and with proper management these parts wear very little. In some cases, with proper attention, these brushes have required no attention or trimming for three months' continual use.

ONE GREAT ADVANTAGE THE VAN DEPOELE DYNAMO POSSESSES IS

that any number or all of the lights may be turned off or on as desired, the current regulating itself to the work to be done; the power consumed to drive the dynamo will at all times correspond to the number of lights or other devices in circuit or in operation. The eighty-light machine runs from eighty arc lights down to three or four, with an exactly corresponding amount of power to the lights in operation.

The lights can be turned off or on with the same ease as gas.

Up to sixteen lights the regulation of the current in the machine is obtained by a peculiar mode of winding; the whole, or any number of lamps can be turned on or off at will; at the same time the machine will produce current only for so many lamps as are burning, consequently the dynamo requires only power corresponding to the work being done. This regulation requires no automatic arrangements whatever, and is perfect in every respect. We call this dynamo the Compensating; in appearance it is like the other dynamos shown. For larger dynamos, from twenty to seventy or eighty lights in one circuit, the regulation leaves nothing to be desired — in all cases the machines only taking power according to the number of lamps burning. The regulation of these machines can be accomplished by hand or automatically. The hand regulation is used wherever the same or nearly the same number of lights are usually burning; a current indicator shows at all times the current strength, and by turning the brushes either up or down on the commutator, the production of current can be varied at will. However, in cases where the number of lights run on the same line is often varied, an automatic current regulator can be applied to the machines, as shown in Fig. 1. This device controls the production of current to perfection, without the slightest manual attention.

In the Van Depoele system of arc lighting, great care has been exercised to keep the electro-motive force of the current down as low as possible, reducing to a minimum the danger attending the operation of large plants. Even with our largest machines, any lamp, or any part of the circuit may be touched with impunity, and never yet have we met with an accident caused through the current of our machines—something which very few companies can boast of. Thus the current of these machines, being of low tension and great quantity (intensity), burns short arcs in the lamps, producing an absolutely white light, reproducing perfectly the solar spectrum; whereas, in all other lights, where high tension is used, and long arcs kept up, the color of the light is decidedly purple or bluish, and although the violet rays hurting the eye, and appearing to be brighter than the yellow, yet on photometric test it will invariably be found that the short arc and the yellow rays have at least twenty-five per cent more dispersive power than the violet. Another advantage of our short-arc system is that our light is perfectly steady, while the long arc of other systems keeps the light dancing and fluttering around continually, to the great discomfort of those under its rays.

With our light the slightest difference in shade of color can be detected as easily as in daylight, something which cannot be done by the high tension or violet lights. A high tension current is not only dangerous to handle, but bursts frequently through the armature, burning out sections and putting the machine out of use until repaired. This difficulty does not exist in our low tension machines, which is certainly not to be overlooked, since the life of the machine is thereby lengthened.

In rainy weather and with good insulation, if one ventures to touch a lamp or other part of the circuit of high tension current, if he is not killed he will receive such a terrible shaking up as to teach him thereafter to stay within respectable distance from the lamp; whereas, with our system and low current no danger whatever exists in handling the lamp or the lines, even in a drenching rain.

THE VAN DEPOELE NEW STANDARD ARC LAMP.

The principal features of this lamp (see Fig. 5) are two electro-magnets,
one in the main and one in the shunt circuit; to the latter is hinged a soft-
iron armature, the free end of which moves
under the influence of the opposite pole of the

FIG. 5.   VAN DEPOELE STANDARD LAMP.

FIG. 6.   VAN DEPOELE UNIVERSAL
LAMP.

main magnet.   This armature carries the carbon lifter, so that any motion
imparted to the armature, under the influence of its electro-magnets, is directly
communicated to the lifter, either separating the carbons or allowing the same

to feed. One other and most important feature of this lamp is that it needs no adjustment after it is made, thus doing away with all tampering by attendants, which has in many cases caused the failure, within a short time, of a good many plants. This lamp is provided with an automatic and hand cut-out, so that any lamp can be cut out or in circuit without affecting the others. All parts of this lamp are very plain, and are not many; but are all made absolutely accurate with special machinery. All parts are interchangeable. Not a single delicate part being present in the whole lamp, it will stand all the tests to which an electric arc lamp can be subjected, without getting out of order. The workmanship cannot be surpassed; the design is simple and neat.

Fig. 6 represents the Van Depoele Universal Lamp. This lamp is intended to be used wherever an ordinary lamp could not be introduced successfully—on high and exposed places, such as towers and the like, or in places where there is much dust, dampness, etc. This lamp has no rod, the carbons being held in place and fed by an endless copper belt. This belt is actuated by a small electric motor, simple in construction, and placed on the top of lamp. This lamp can be placed horizontally or turned upside down without in the least affecting the proper feeding of the same. Carbons twenty-four inches long can be used in cases where long-hours run is needed. Our Universal Lamp is certainly the most perfect arc lamp in the market, and is provided, in a nutshell, with all the requirements of a perfect lamp. The same can also be made ornamental if desired.

Fig. 7 shows our Double-Service Hanging Lamp, running sixteen hours without replacing carbons, and is intended to be used in shops or other places where all-night illumination is required. All parts are simple, solid, and not liable to get out of order.

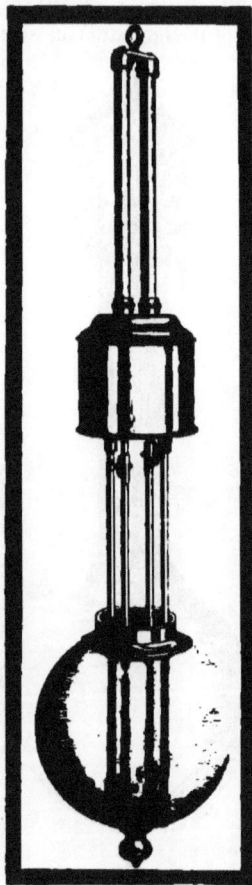

FIG. 7. DOUBLE SERVICE HANGING LAMP.

Fig. 8 shows our Double Lamp, sixteen hours' service, intended to be placed on high poles, such as are used in street lighting, etc. This lamp is provided with a solid frame by which it is held in position; in other particulars it is similar to the one shown in Fig. 7.

Fig. 9 shows a very convenient and safe means for raising and lowering lamps to replace the carbons. It consists of a wooden plate screwed securely to the ceiling. Upon this plate are fastened two pulleys provided with binding posts, to which the circuit wires are connected. Over these pulleys are placed two cables, attached to the lamp binding posts, and to the other free ends are

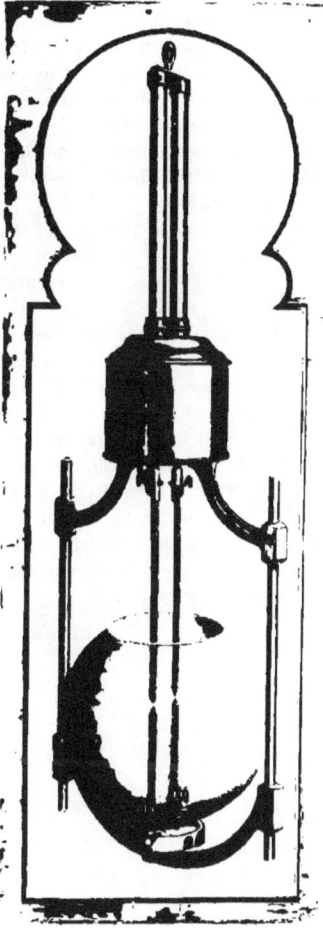

FIG. 8. DOUBLE-SERVICE STREET LAMP.

FIG. 9. LAMP HANGER.

hung weights counterbalancing the lamp, so that the lamp remains at any height you wish to put it. This avoids the carrying around of the step ladder, which is very annoying, especially in much frequented places, such as hotels, etc.

Fig. 10 shows the Van Depoele Patent Automatic Switch, and Current Indicator combined, the whole contained in one frame, with all parts in sight and easy of access. The function of the combination apparatus is: First, to indicate correctly the condition of the current, whether one lamp or the whole number the generator can supply are running, showing at once if anything wrong is going on along the line, or with the generator, so that no matter how long the service line, at any time can the condition of the working circuit be seen

The second function of the apparatus is the automatic switch, in case of accidental breaking of the main or working circuit, the automatic switch lever, which was at first kept down by the electro-magnet in the main circuit, is now carried upward and breaks circuit, with the current, which energizes the fields of the dynamo, thus preventing any further current to be generated, and saving the machine harmless.

FIG. 10.   CURRENT REGULATOR, SWITCH
AND INDICATOR.

FOCUSING LAMPS.

Fig. 11 shows a special headlight and lamp for steamboats and locomotives, warranted to be unaffected by the most severe vibrations. The peculiarities of this lamp are that the carbons are fed and regulated by an electric motor contained in the lamp. No delicate parts are present, and no adjustment whatever is needed to the lamp. When the dynamo runs with normal speed it is impossible to keep the carbons at any other distance apart while emitting light, than that to which the lamp is made. On putting the carbons together, they are immediately separated, while, when pulled apart further than the normal distance, they will be moved toward each other until the proper distance is obtained. The feed of the carbons is most perfect, consequently a perfectly steady light is the result. The lamp is inclosed in a neat and solid case, and is so arranged that it can be turned to any angle desired ; for this purpose the lamp

FIG. 11. STEAMBOAT HEADLIGHT

and case are carried by a rotary platform, and so arranged that it can be worked by the wheelsman or pilot from his post. The Van Depoele Company manufac-

ture especially for steamboats a portable lamp, which can be hung up in a few
moments in any part of the boat, or can be placed on shore if needed. This
lamp is provided with the same feeding mechanism as the preceding lamp, and
can be run for from eight to sixteen hours without renewal of carbons. This
lamp is in general appearance similar to Fig. 6.

Fig. 12 shows the Focusing Lamp for the use of the lecture room. The lamp is
mounted upon a very solid stand, and can be moved horizontally and vertically to
any desired angle. The working of the lamp is perfect and reliable, and any candle
power can be given, from five hundred to

FIG. 12.   FOCUSING LAMP FOR LECTURE
ROOMS, ETC.

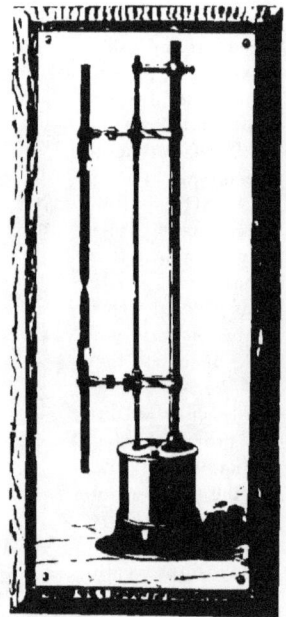

FIG. 13.   HEADLIGHT FOCUSING
LAMPS.

twenty thousand or more. The reflectors used in conjunction with these lamps
have to be chosen to correspond with the work to be done. Any range from one
mile to ten can be furnished, or manufactured to order.

Fig. 13 represents the Focusing Lamp proper, as is contained in the case
shown in Fig. 11.

POWER REQUIRED TO RUN THE ELECTRIC LIGHT.

The power required to drive a dynamo will be in direct proportion to the number and the size of lights given, although some machines take a great deal more power than others. In some machines the construction of the armature is such that the heat produced in the iron core would in a short time burn the insulation of the copper conductor around the same, were it not that some ventilating device is used to keep the high temperature down, some armatures being made very much like blowing fans. The power spent in producing this air blast is an absolute loss; it is avoided and not at all needed in the Van Depoele dynamo. Our armature after a sixteen hours' run is as cool as when started. Thus it will be seen that this is one cause at least which will account for the difference in power required to produce a certain amount of current. The following are a few facts, giving an idea of the power our machines take and how they compare with others:

A test was made in our works with three forty-light dynamos, driven by an engine with a 12 x 12 cylinder, at two hundred and fifty revolutions per minute, the dynamos running at a speed of seven hundred revolutions per minute. One machine was turned on after another, and one hundred and twenty lights like stars were blazing for over an hour while the test lasted. This engine is rated by the company manufacturing the same as ninety horse-power.

In the Milwaukee Industrial Exposition, where we have sixty large-size arc lights, run by a Reynolds-Corliss engine, cards were taken a number of times, and indicated invariably forty-five horse-power for the sixty lights.

In the Sherman House, Chicago, where this company has a twenty-light plant, a large number of cards has been taken, and the average power is fifteen horse-power for the twenty lights.

In J. V. Farwell & Co.'s, Chicago, cards have been taken by Mr. Morovia, Civil Engineer, indicating that the forty-light machines require very nearly three-quarters horse-power per light, or thirty horse-power for the forty lights. The twenty-five-light machines in the same place show also an average of three-quarters horse-power per light.

In electric lighting reference is often made to the power consumed by a dynamo, and a number of lights, without even attempting to state what kind of current, or power of light is used. In some instances novices are persuaded or misled in their own work, claiming to have found the philosopher's stone in electric lighting, that is, to run a certain number of lights, with an astonishingly small amount of power. Now, if the matter be inquired into, and strength and quantity of current measured, it will be found that really nothing new has been accomplished. Intensity and tension in electricity are two factors which will explain themselves to those versed in the art. In electrical as well as in steam and hydraulic engineering, positive calculations can be made to-day which will at once put down these extraordinary claims. To make matters clear, let us admit that we have a tank delivering water through different sizes of pipe, and at the delivery of these pipes, we rate the pressure to be one hundred pounds. It will

2

now be understood that the one-fourth-inch pipe will furnish less water than the inch. The tension or pressure is the same in both cases, but the quantity varies, and so it is in electricity. We may have the same tension in two different machines, but their quantity will vary. We may be able to run say twenty arc lights, with ten horse-power, or even less, with one dynamo, whereas another dynamo, running also twenty lights, will take from fifteen to eighteen horse-power. We admit that the dynamos here used are both as perfect in proportions and principle as is possible to make them. Then it will be understood that the twenty arc lights, consuming ten horse-power, cannot have the same current as the other twenty lights, consuming fifteen horse-power, and consequently cannot produce the same amount of light. The fact is that in the first case we get a high tension and small quantity, whereas in the second case we get the same tension, but a correspondingly larger quantity of current. Were this not true, perpetual motion would no longer be an impossibility, but much more than that, for by first starting one of these mysterious dynamos it would run another much more powerful, which dynamo would run one still more powerful, etc. Mother nature is good, but has never given forth a plant without seed, food and time. Electric lights cannot be produced without the current of electricity, and are in proportion to the kind of current made use of.

RECOMMENDATIONS FOR POWER TO OPERATE DYNAMO ELECTRIC MACHINES FOR ELECTRIC LIGHTING.

Without regard to description, whether steam, water, gas or other power supplied, there should be an abundance,— say, one-fourth more than what the dynamo really takes. This will prove most economical, and insure good results. Never should any attempt be made to run electric lights where there is lack of power; it is simply waste of time, useless expense, and of course general dissatisfaction.

In selecting engines for electric lighting, none but the very best should be adopted. The price may be somewhat higher than the common engines, but ample reward will be given by the superior results obtained. Since electric lighting has come in vogue, steam engineers have turned their attention to the want, and very fine engines have been brought in the market, especially of the high-speed class, which is best fit for running either arc or incandescent lights. Another and important item is, that steam should be kept as near as practicable at even pressure. In cases where the power is taken from a main shaft of a shop, it should be steady, since variation of speed will produce variation of current, and all will reflect in the light.

When the speed of a dynamo has been determined, it should be kept there as near as possible. It is in all cases advisable to use independent power to drive electric-light machinery. The speed will be regular, and the light can be run while the machinery is at rest. Let it be remembered that the current in a dynamo corresponds exactly with the power which drives it. When the power is steady the current will be steady, and perfect success is secured.

ELECTRICAL TRANSMISSION OF POWER.

The Van Depoele dynamo is peculiarly adapted to the transmission of power. In trials made during the month of February, 1883, a motor weighing three hundred pounds was placed on a car capable of carrying twenty-five people; a similar dynamo was run at the works, which furnished, by means of copper conductors, the current to operate the motor on the car. Trials were made for several days, and with perfect success. The car, being filled to its utmost capacity, was run back and forward with the utmost ease. The incline of the track varied from one-eighth to five-eighths inch to the foot, the car and its load being often stopped on the steepest incline, and held there for a time, and then again started up grade with the utmost facility, the motor responding with promptitude to the manipulation of the switch, by means of which the direction of motion is reversed and the power controlled. During the Inter-State Industrial Exposition held at Chicago, in the fall of 1883, an elevated railway car was run, and with a control that convinced the most skeptical. Thousands of people have enjoyed the ride every day of the show. Another illustration of the transmission of power might not be out of the way here. In the month of November, 1883, one day about 11:50 A.M., the engine running our factory broke down completely, the piston rod becoming disengaged from the cross head, smashing things around generally. No sooner

FIG. 14. VAN DEPOELE MOTOR.

FIG. 15. BATTERY FOR SMALL MOTORS.

was the situation taken in than a thirty-horse-power generator was put in place so as to be driven by the independent engine, which is only used for testing machines and lamps, but not at all in communication with the shafting of the factory. A second machine or motor was placed in position, so that from its pulley a belt was run to a pulley on the factory shaft. Two No. 6 wires were now run from generator to motor, and from motor back to generator. The generator was started by the testing engine, and immediately the motor, which was belted to the main shaft driving the machinery, started up, and was put at proper speed. All this was done in about thirty minutes, and at 12:30 P.M. the factory was running as usual, and this lasted for over three weeks, until the engine had been repaired. During all this time the power was perfectly steady, and no attention but a few drops of oil was required to the motor. We may safely state that it is only a question of a short time when the distribution of power by electricity will become general. In a great many instances where water power is available, advantage can be taken to transmit power over great distances. This company also manufactures electric motors of all sizes, from a sewing machine motor up to any desired horse-power required.

Fig. 14 represents a small motor intended for sewing machines, or other light work.

Fig. 15 shows the battery used to run it.

For large motors, the pattern is similar to our ordinary dynamo, as shown in Fig. 1.

We are prepared to put up plants for the electrical transmission of power from one horse-power to one hundred, and over.

ELECTRO PLATING.

This company manufactures electro-plating machines of any capacity required, and a stock of regular sizes is constantly kept on hand. We claim that this machine has fewer parts than any dynamo ever made. Simplicity in such apparatus should commend itself. There are two brushes, and these can run for weeks without the slightest attention. By a very simple arrangement the current strength can be brought up or down to suit the kind of work, as well as the amount. We furnish an indicator with these machines, which indicates exactly the current strength. This serves as a guide to the plater.

These machines do not require water nor anything of the kind, and do not heat under the heaviest work. The current can be so regulated without resistance boxes, or anything outside of the machines, as to make either a slow or fast deposit. The deposit is exceedingly fine and tough, so that for electrotyping it is not necessary to make as thick a shell as is required with a brittle deposit.

FIG. 16. VAN DEPOELE ELECTRO-PLATING MACHINE

We manufacture also plating machines to order, for special purposes.

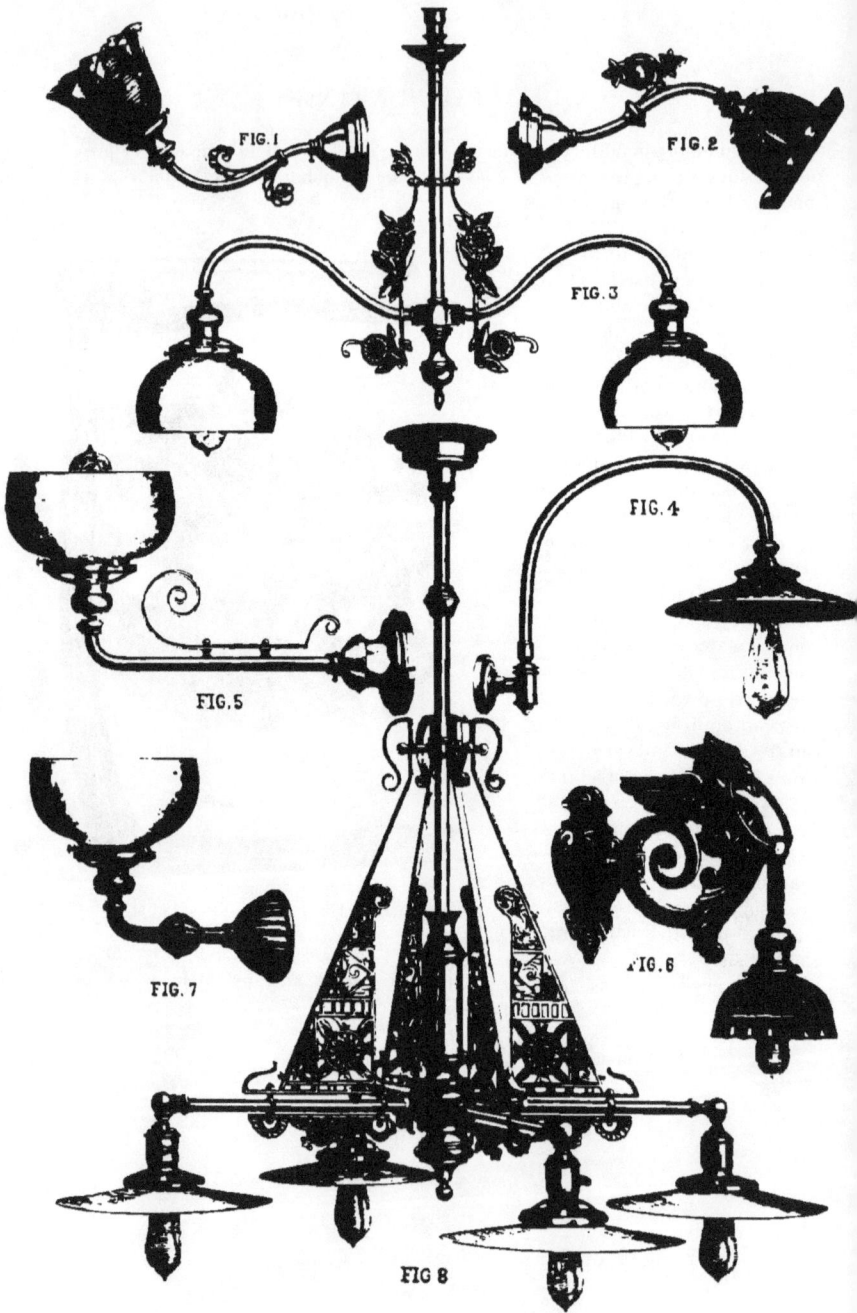

FIG.1
FIG.2
FIG. 3
FIG. 4
FIG.5
FIG. 6
FIG. 7
FIG 8

LIGHTING BY INCANDESCENCE.

Lighting by incandescence is certainly not economical as compared with arc lighting.   In the arc-lighting system we easily produce two thousand candle-power per horse-power, whereas with the best dynamo and lamps made no more than one hundred and sixty candle-power per horse-power has been obtained, or about *one-twelfth of what is obtained by the arc.* Still people will have incandescent light, if it costs as much as gas, or even a trifle more. The superiority of incandescent lighting over gas is, to-day, too well known to discuss the same here. For theaters, churches, etc., or even stores and dwelling houses, the incandescent light can be used successfully. However, for large areas we recommend the use of the arc light, it being far the cheapest, as above stated. Whenever parties desire to have a few incandescent lights placed in the office, from our arc lamp circuit, we can give them; but as soon as it is worth while, say for one hundred to five hundred lights, it is preferable to have a separate plant, which will work more economically than in case of arc and incandescents in one circuit. Our mode of distributing the current is entirely novel, and can be extended on as long lines as arc-light circuits with a conductor not heavier than No. 4 copper wire, while in all other systems very heavy and expensive copper conductors have to be used.

FIG. 17.   INCANDESCENT LAMP.

THE VAN DEPOELE PATENTS.

Most of the patents granted in the United States on electric lighting have been for special construction. This company have used great care in applying for patents, to patent only something *new*, and on as broad principles as possible. The company own the Van Depoele patents for the United States for electric lights and power, and claim, without fear of successful contradiction, to cover more *new* matter than is embraced in the patents of any other company. Our light systems, lamps, dynamos and appliances, are entirely different from others. *We do not infringe the valid patents of any other company*, but have distinctive systems of our own. Some companies attempt to force their inferior goods upon

the market by pretending that parties purchasing other plants will be sued for
infringing their patents. This we have not done, but shall take measures to
protect our patents by legal proceedings against the parties manufacturing.

ADVANTAGES WE CLAIM OVER ALL OTHERS.

1st. That our whole system is the most simple in construction and operation.
Our aim ever has been to do away with complication so far as possible. Our
dynamo is the most simple in the market, and that its efficiency stands higher than
any other, we are ready to demonstrate at any time by practical test.

2nd. Our lamp has fewer parts than any lamp before the public, and is the
result of years of study and practice. Our lamps have, in a nutshell, all that is
necessary to form a perfect arc lamp. After the lamps leave the shop no adjustment is necessary, nor can they be adjusted or tampered with; we use no dash
pots nor glycerine, to spill and give an everlasting bother.

3rd. With all our dynamos, the full capacity, or part, can be made available,
and only so much current is produced as is wanted. To effect this, we have
both hand and automatic regulation, working to perfection. In all cases the
power consumed is in proportion to the number of lights or other devices, such
as motors, etc., in circuit.

4th. The brushes on our dynamos are very simple and easily put in place,
and in many instances have run for three months without trimming, no spark
being present between the commutator and brushes. We need not blow it back
with an air force pump, as in some systems.

5th. The construction of our armature is perfect in every particular, and
under the heaviest work does not heat in the least, although we use no air blast
to keep its temperature down, as in many other armatures, which thus waste a
good deal of power in trying to get rid of the heat, which costs power to produce. By this construction we are enabled to make dynamos of almost any
capacity without endangering the insulation and the life of our machines.

6th. We manufacture really the most powerful arc-light dynamo in the market, the capacity being of eighty 2000-candle-power lights. Its management is
as easy as a four-light dynamo, and never have we heard nor had the slightest
trouble with these machines.

7th. For the transmission of power by electricity, we claim to have the most
perfect method in existence, for regulation and control of the same, either for
tramway or stationary use. Our dynamo is peculiarly adapted to the transmission of power, as we have had occasion to show repeatedly.

8th. We claim that owing to the perfect construction of our machines, and
the true principles upon which the whole of our system of lighting is based,
we produce results that can not be beaten by any of our competitors.

9th. For distinguishing colors, there is no light on the market to-day, better
fitted than ours. The tension and quantity of our current is so balanced as to
produce very little of the violet rays, while with most other lights which are of

too high a tension, they keep on flaming and flickering with a purple hue. For photography, our light is more actinic than any in use to-day.

10th. Extreme simplicity in construction in all parts of the system; no intricate machinery nor delicate devices being used.

11th. Ease of management and attendance to dynamo while in operation.

12th. Perfect control of the current to run a given number of lights from one up to the full capacity of the machine.

13th. Perfect safety in handling the lamps while the current is on.

14th. The light produced is absolutely white and steady.

15th. The almost total absence of the violet rays makes our light more diffusive than any other.

16th. The amount of power required to drive the machines and produce a *certain amount of light* is the lowest on record, and this we are ready to demonstrate at any time.

17th. Having fewer parts to our dynamos than any other machine made, the wear and tear is reduced to a minimum.

18th. In places where a large amount of light is wanted, our light is certainly cheaper than gas, and the larger the plant the more economical the light.

19th. The Van Depoele light can be looked at with impunity, and seems rather to improve the eye than to produce harm, as is the case with a flickering light.

20th. The whole of the apparatus is made of the best material obtainable, the workmanship is thorough in all particulars. This accounts for the great success of our plants. Not one single plant of ours has been out of use a day for over a year.

THE ADAMS TOWER.

This company is prepared to give estimates for, and erect any kind of towers desired. The above tower or mast is the invention of F. U. Adams, of Chicago, and is probably the cheapest form of iron mast that can be made. These towers are manufactured by the Adams Tower Co., 203 Van Buren street, Chicago.

ADVANTAGES OF TOWER LIGHTING.

Van Depoele Electric Light Co., Chicago, Ill.:

GENTLEMEN,—In reply to your late favor, inquiring about our system of lighting this city, I would say, after a careful trial of over three months, the system of elevating the lights by the use of towers is pronounced by all who have studied results a great success. My best judgment is that to light our city equally as well as it is now lighted would require 120 lamps, if placed on poles, as against 29 now used on towers; in other words, one light on a tower is equal in value to four lights on poles, and this difference indicates fairly the economy of the tower system for city lighting or for parks.

I assume that properly lighted streets are an important feature in a well regulated city or village, for upon this depends very materially the comfort, convenience and safety of the citizens. How can this best be done? We have passed through the various stages of the primitive systems, and many of our progressive cities have adopted the electric light, while numerous others are considering the subject. It will be found that a given area can be lighted by electricity at a less cost than the same area can be equally lighted by gas. Various plans are in use for distributing the lights. One is to support the burners on poles of different heights, say 18 to 25 feet, standing on street corners; another, to string a wire across the street and suspend the lamps therefrom, 25 feet above the street; another, to erect towers from 100 to 250 feet high, which support a group of lamps; and still another method is an arch sprung over the street, where one lamp will light, say, two blocks, or 800 feet in four directions from the light. In this latter system the lamp is suspended 35 feet above the ground, not too high to lose any light, but high enough to remove the unpleasant and almost blinding glare of the light which occurs when the lamps are immediately in front of passers on the sidewalk. The tower system, so well illustrated in Elgin in connection with the Van Depoele light, produces universally good results. There is a sufficient accumulation of light at a proper elevation to give a truly beautiful and natural effect. An average city two miles square can be elegantly illuminated with thirty-five 2,000-candle-power lamps, elevated 100 to 150 feet on, say, seven or more towers, as may be desirable, for $7,500 per annum. It now costs to light the city of Washington with gas $130,000 per year. To light that city with electric lights would require about three hundred 2,000-candle-power lamps, placed on forty towers 150 feet high, and would cost about $100,000. The city would be illuminated in a superb manner at a saving of $30,000 per year over the present plan. The relative expense of the two systems of lighting is thus well shown. It is not to be wondered at then that, in addition to the many cities that have adopted the electric light, numerous others are investigating it, and are almost sure to "fall into line," and it looks to us as though the electric light must soon come into general use by reason of its superiority and real economy. It need hardly be said that the light in Elgin, and the manner of its distribution, find almost universal commendation; and yet the opposition to the tower system was at first really bitter, and was found in the various electric-light companies as well as outside of them. The success in Elgin has almost entirely overcome the local prejudice, and the tower system stands preëminent as the one for city lighting. Elgin has seven towers, of which six are 125 feet in height and one 150 feet. On them is a total number of twenty-nine lamps of 2,000-candle-power. The city contracts with the electric-light company (which owns the entire plant, towers and all) for five years, at $6,800 per year. The lamps are to burn at least 300 nights per year, and as many more as the condition of things may require. As expressions of popular and well considered opinion on the question of the real merit of the electric light, I send you a few quotations from letters received, all tending to show its universal appreciation, as follows:

Mr. Jennings, Superintendent Buffalo Company, says "Considering the quantity and quality of light, it is by all odds cheapest to light by electricity."

Mr. Moore, Superintendent, Springfield, Mass., writes "It is cheaper in any city that was fairly lighted before; in quality it is immeasurably superior, it affords increased protection to those using roads and sidewalks, and for police purposes it is of great value "

Mr. Orton, Bay City, Mich., says "Considering amount of light furnished, and area lighted, it would cost a great deal more to light with gas."

Mr. Stannard, of Nashville, Tenn., writes "Considering all the advantages attached to the light, we consider it at sixty cents per light, per night, more economical than gas at $1.05 per thousand feet."

Alleghany Light Company, Pittsburgh, says "The price of gas to private consumers is one dollar per thousand feet, to the city, seventy-five cents per thousand feet. From this you can see we have considerable opposition in this direction."

Superintendent, Manchester, N. H., writes "We light three bridges seven hundred and sixty-five feet long each, with two lamps to a bridge. Can tell time by a watch on any part of them, the darkest night The cost of lighting a city with electric light, as it should be lighted, would be some more than it would be with gas, but the light would be enough better to make up the difference."

Treasurer of the company at Lynn, Mass., writes. "The arc light is unquestionably the very best and most economical light for large spaces. We light a large hall with eight arc lights twice as well as it was formerly lighted with three hundred and sixty gas jets, and at much less expense."

The question really is, can the people afford to dispense with the electric light? We think not.

Yours, truly,

Elgin, Illinois, May 10, 1884.   GEORGE S. BOWEN.

Dr. J. F. Boynton, of Syracuse, N. Y., telling of his six weeks' trip in the Western country, says:

"At Elgin, Illinois, I was not only interested in their watch factory, and their factory for condensing milk, in a superior way, but also in their magnificent system of illumination. They have the tower system of electric lighting. The effect produced is that of half moonlight over every part of the city. There are seven towers with several lanterns on each tower, each light of 2,000 candle power. By this system none of the dazzling glaring effects, and the contrast of gloom and brightness, which characterize low lighting, is seen, but the radiance is soft and diffused, which is the best for protection, safety and general usefulness. The light on each tower extends over a radius of 2,000 feet, and can be seen for several miles. Elgin claims to be the best lighted city in the world, and is just now attracting great attention on that account. The Hon. George S. Bowen, who has had charge of the work, has done it in a most satisfactory manner."—*From Syracuse Herald, April 27, 1884.*

LIST OF PATENTS.

The following are some of the patents granted to Charles J. Van Depoele, owned by our Company, besides a large number now pending:

No. 227,078, April 27, 1880. Improvements in Electric Lights.
No. 232,574, September 21, 1880. Dynamo Electric Machines.
No. 247,278, September 20, 1881. Dynamo Electric Machines.
No. 257,990, May 16, 1882. Combined Electric Motor and Generator.
No. 257,989, May 16, 1882. Electric Arc Lamps.
No. 257,988, May 16, 1882. Shunting Device for Electric Lamp.
No. 259,061, June 6, 1882. Dynamo Electric Machines.
No. 259,062, June 6, 1882. Electric Lamps.
No. 261,280, July 18, 1882. Electric Arc Lamps.
No. 262,333, August 8, 1882. Electric Arc Lamps.
No. 266,735, October 31, 1882. Inductoriums.
No. 270,352, January 9, 1883. Devices for Controlling Electrical Currents.
No. 275,549, April 10, 1883. Dynamo Electric Machines.
No. 276,099, April 17, 1883. Storage or Secondary Batteries.
No. 282,414, July 31, 1883. Secondary Electric Batteries, etc.
No. 284,779, September 11. Retort for Carbonizing Incandescents.
No. 285,528, September 25. Regulator for Electrical Apparatus.
No. 285,529, September 25. Secondary Battery.
No. 285,527, September 25. Device for Adjusting Brushes for Dynamo-Electric Machine.
No. 285,857, October 2. Electric Motor.
No. 285,858, October 2. Electric Railway.
No. 285,859, October 2. Automatic Electric Circuit Changer.
No. 286,093, October 2. Electric Lamp.
No. 286,094, October 2. Electric Arc Lamp.
No. 287,343, October 23, 1883. Regulators for Dynamo-Electric Machines.
No. 287,344, October 23, 1883. Electrodes for Electric Arc Lamps.
No. 287,345, October 23, 1883. Safety Switches for Dynamo-Electric Machines.
No. 287,346, October 23, 1883. Insulating Material for Dynamo Machines.
No. 287,347, October 23, 1883. System of Generating and Distributing Electric Currents.
No. 288,682, November 20, 1883. Safety Cut-outs for Electric Lamps.
No. 291,553, January 8, 1884. Electric Arc Lamps.
No. 291,554, January 8, 1884. Regulators for Dynamo-Electric Machines.
No. 291,648, January 8, 1884. Electric Circuit Closer.
No. 291,649, January 8, 1884. Electric Safety Cut-outs.
No. 291,650, January 8, 1884. Current Regulators for Electric Motors.
No. 291,651, January 8, 1884. Electric Lamps.
No. 291,652, January 8, 1884. Safety Cut-outs for Series of Electric Lamps.

No. 291,653, January 8, 1884. Electric Arc Lamps.

No. 294,165, February 26, 1884. Motors for Electric Regulators.

No. 294,532, March 4, 1884. Electric Arc Lamps.

No. 294,533, March 4, 1884. Electric Arc Lamps.

No. 297,878, April 24, 1884. Dynamo Electric Machines.

No. 298,431, May 13, 1884. Inductorium for Running Motors and Incandescent and Arc Lights on same circuit.

IMPROVEMENTS.

It is often asked whether there will not be some improvements made, so as to furnish light at a much reduced cost of power. To this we must say that some improvements will be made, but they will simply be to details of fixtures, of regulation and attachments, but not to generation. Dynamo machines are now perfectly understood, and are very perfect apparatus, as they really convert from eighty to ninety-five per cent of the motive power in available current, to be used outside of the generator, either for lighting or other purposes. In arc-light systems there is much need of a carbon which will be of a more even density, and a purer article. This want is known, and scientists are searching for better results, and real progress is constantly being made in this direction. The same may be said with regard to incandescent lamps, which are being very rapidly improved and made more durable.

Nevertheless, every now and then we find in our dailies that some great discovery has been made which (will) revolutionize the whole electrical science. Some go even so far as to assert that electricity will be produced without expenditure of energy. These absurd and impossible statements are often enough to mislead the general public, and more than once have capitalists been badly fleeced by these pretending schemers, who unscrupulously make their business of enriching themselves by the most dishonest practices.

Those who contemplate to use electricity, for lighting or other purposes, can without risk apply to some responsible company, and may feel assured that it costs no more to produce electricity to-day than it will cost in one hundred years hence. As has been stated elsewhere, electricity is understood as well to-day as is steam engineering, and perfect calculations can be made in both cases. Let it be remembered that since the first condensing engine of Watt till to-day, no more economical engine has been built, although a good many improvements have been made in the workmanship and general construction of such engines; but to-day, with the very best of apparatus, it takes as much steam to operate an engine of a certain horse-power as it did in the days of the immortal Watt. The same will hold good for electrical machines; so that the improvements expected will simply be in such or other detail; but very little or nothing is left to secure a cheaper production of current than the means now at command.

PRICE LIST FOR VAN DEPOELE ELECTRIC LIGHT APPARATUS.

SUBJECT TO CHANGE WITHOUT NOTICE.

PRICES ON DYNAMO ELECTRIC MACHINES ONLY.

Sizes.	No. of Lights.	Diam. of Pulley.	Width of Belt.	Revolutions per Min.*	Price.
No. 0	1	6 inches	2 inches	1,200	$............
" 1	1	7 "	2 "	1,200	....
" 2	2	8 "	2½ "	1,100	
" 3	3	9 "	2½ "	1,000	
" 4	4	10 "	2½ "	1,000	
" 5	5	10 "	3 "	1,050	
" 6	6	10 "	3 "	1,050	
" 8	8	11 "	3½ "	1,050	
" 10	10	11 "	4½ "	1,025	
" 12	12	12 "	4½ "	1,000	
" 16	16	14 "	5½ "	1,000	
" 20	20	16 "	6½ "	9,000	....
" 30	30	18 "	8½ "	850	....
" 40	40	24 "	10 "	800	....
" 60	60	26 "	12 "	700	....

* Only approximate speed and power required can be given on general list; these depend on the intensity of light desired and distance of lamps from machine. The smallest machines require about one horse-power per lamp, but the larger machines need much less proportionately. Endless belts should be used, and should be of very best quality. Double belts are preferable and last longer, besides remaining true.

PRICES ON ELECTRIC LAMPS.

Van Depoele "Standard" Lamp............................ $............
Sixteen-Hour Service Lamp ....
Universal Lamp, sixteen hours' service ....
Headlight Lamp only.......................................
Headlight Lamp, with Parabolic Reflector and Case..........
Focusing Lamp, for Camera and Class Use, with Stand....... ....

Reflectors (of any size) for diffusing or concentrating the light, made to order.
Plain Conducting Wire ....per lb. ....c.
Insulated Conducting Wire .... " ....c.
Insulated Cable.................................... " ....c.
Globes — Plain, Ground and Opal ....c.

The cost of running the above will be from one to two cents per hour for the carbons consumed in each lamp, the expense depending on quality and size of lights. Estimates furnished on application.

Address all communications to

VAN DEPOELE ELECTRIC LIGHT CO.,

CHICAGO, ILL.

TESTIMONIALS.

JOHN V. FARWELL & CO., CHICAGO, NEW YORK, MANCHESTER, PARIS.
CHICAGO, May 26, 1884.

VAN DEPOELE ELECTRIC LIGHT CO., CHICAGO:
   Gentlemen,—We are using your light to light our wholesale dry-goods establishment in this city. It gives us satisfaction, and we can recommend it to those wanting electric lights.
                                                    JOHN V. FARWELL & CO.

MAYOR'S OFFICE,
FREEPORT, ILL., August 6, 1883.

PRESIDENT VAN DEPOELE ELECTRIC LIGHT CO.:
   Dear Sir,—The Van Depoele light has been used in our city since December last, and has given splendid satisfaction. The parties that are using it are more than pleased, and new lights are going in every day. I have investigated the different electric lights, having been on several committees for that purpose, and am free to say that the Van Depoele, in my opinion, lays over all other electric lights.   Yours respectfully,   JAS. McNAMARA, Mayor.

ABBOTT BUGGY CO., WHOLESALE CARRIAGE MANUFACTURERS,
CHICAGO, ILL., August 3, 1883.

PRESIDENT VAN DEPOELE ELECTRIC LIGHT CO.:
   Dear Sir,—Your system of lights in our machine shop answers the purpose admirably. They have run night and day without any trouble or annoyance.   Yours truly,
                                                    ABBOTT BUGGY CO.

LEROY PAYNE, PALMER HOUSE LIVERY.
CHICAGO, August 3, 1883.

PRESIDENT VAN DEPOELE ELECTRIC LIGHT CO.:
   Dear Sir,—In answer to your inquiry in regard to the plant placed by you in my stables, I will say that it is entirely satisfactory, and that you have done all that you agreed to, and should be perfectly willing that you should refer any one wishing such a plant to me.
                      Respectfully yours,   LEROY PAYNE.

STEAMER "GAZELLE," HENRY BABY, Proprietor.
CHICAGO, August 4, 1883.

PRESIDENT VAN DEPOELE ELECTRIC LIGHT CO.:
   Dear Sir,—We are using the Van Depoele Electric Light upon our steamer, the "Gazelle," with great satisfaction. For the lighting of boats, docks or wharves, I consider it the best light in the world, and I know whereof I speak.   HENRY BABY, Proprietor and Manager.

OFFICE OF THORN WIRE HEDGE CO., MANUFACTURERS OF KELLY BARB WIRE,
CHICAGO, August 6, 1883.

VAN DEPOELE ELECTRIC LIGHT CO.,
   We have had in our shop for the past two years a Van Depoele Electric Light plant of sixteen lights. It has given us perfect satisfaction, and has cost us scarcely anything for repairs. It has been run days all the time, and at least one-half the time day and night. Our lights are in dark rooms, where the machines could not be run before we got the lights; now the workmen prefer to work in those rooms. We consider the Van Depoele superior to anything we have seen.
                      THORN WIRE HEDGE CO., by W. A. STILES, Secretary.

R. R. MEREDITH & SONS, ELECTROTYPERS AND PRINTERS OF MUSIC,
CHICAGO, August 7, 1883.

PRESIDENT VAN DEPOELE ELECTRIC LIGHT CO.:
   Dear Sir,—Your electro-plating machine we have been using the last three months has been doing first-class work, giving us entire satisfaction, and especially remarkable for the beautiful deposit it makes, and would cheerfully recommend it to any one needing such a machine. Our dealings with your company have been most satisfactory.
                      Respectfully,   R. R. MEREDITH & SONS.

August 7, 1883.

To Whom It may Concern:

This is to testify that I am running for Messrs. R. R. Meredith & Sons, an electro-plating machine of the Van Depoele system, and I must say that the machine gives me perfect satisfaction. I can regulate the same with perfect ease to do either a large or small amount of work. The shell is perfectly smooth and tough. Have no trouble with rotten or burned copper, and no copper drops in battery. I can with perfect ease get out twelve plates, 18 x 20 inches, in two hours, and during the nine years of my experience with other machines, I have not been able to produce the above result in less than from four to six hours. I never have had the slightest trouble running the machine, either for a small or large number of plates. I prefer to work with this machine to any other I know. JOHN LEHMAN, Electro-plater.

A. Plamondon Manufacturing Co., Chas. A. Plamondon, Sup't.

Chicago, August 9, 1883.

President Van Depoele Electric Light Co.:

Dear Sir,—We have a sixteen-light plant of the Van Depoele system in our establishment, which has been working for about six months without any interruption whatever, and without a single cent expended for repairs. With it we are enabled to utilize every foot of space in our foundry and shops with greater economy than we can by daylight. We are entirely satisfied with the steadiness and brilliancy of the light — likewise its economy. We searched the field of electric lighting over quite thoroughly before purchasing, and selected the Van Depoele system entirely on account of its steadiness and great diffusiveness. For the lighting of large areas we consider it without an equal to-day. The cost to us of operating our lights is simply nominal, as we already had steam power in our shops, which is now running the machinery in the shops, as well as the electric lights. It requires less than a horse-power per light for the sixteen lights.

Very respectfully, A. PLAMONDON MANUF'G. CO.

CHAS. A. PLAMONDON, Superintendent.

Steamer "City Winona," J. C. Follmer, Captain.

Winona, Minn., August 12, 1883.

President Van Depoele Electric Light Co.:

Dear Sir,—I am satisfied from what I have seen of lights on steamboats, that the one you put on our boat is the best on the river, and I would gladly recommend it to any one.

Respectfully, J. C. FOLLMER,

Captain Steamer "City Winona."

Carson, Pirie, Scott & Co.,

Wholesale Dry Goods, Madison and Franklin Sts.,

Chicago, August 9, 1883.

President Van Depoele Electric Light Co.:

Dear Sir,—In reply to yours of the 31st inst., in regard to the working of the Van Depoele plant in our establishment, would say that it is working to our entire satisfaction; and for strength and brilliancy of the lights, we believe they are not surpassed by any others.

Of the twenty-three lamps in circuit we have them all under perfect control, switching them in and out at will. Our run being of ten hours' duration, during the day we are not at all times required to burn the full number of lights, and find the saving of carbons an item by your system of cutting out such as are not needed.

This day being an illustration of the same, only basement lights are needed — eight in number — first, second and third-floor lights are switched out.

As regards the dynamo, our engineer has not the slightest trouble with it, and firmly believes he has the best arc lights in the city.

Have not indicated our engine, but we are in a fair way to do so shortly. Will then furnish you with accurate figures of power required.

Yours very respectfully, CARSON, PIRIE. SCOTT & CO.

Cedar Rapids Electric Light and Power Co.,

Cedar Rapids, Iowa, August 1, 1883.

President Van Depoele Electric Light Co., Chicago, Ill.:

Dear Sir,—Yours of the 31st ult. received. You may quote me in your catalogue for this year as saying with reference to your light:

This company has been operating over fifty Van Depoele lights since January, 1883. We selected this light because we believed it to be superior to any other. We have never regretted our choice. Our patrons have been entirely satisfied with the quality of the light, and we with its economy. Yours truly. C. G. GREENE, Prest.

3

SHERMAN HOUSE, J. IRVING PEARCE, Proprietor,
CHICAGO, ILL., July 31, 1883.

PRESIDENT VAN DEPOELE ELECTRIC LIGHT CO.:
Gents,— I am using a 20-light electric-light plant of your patent and manufacture. I think your light has no superior, if it has any equal.
Yours truly,   J. IRVING PEARCE.

CHICAGO, May 21, 1883.

PRESIDENT VAN DEPOELE ELECTRIC LIGHT CO., CHICAGO, ILL.:
Dear Sir,— We wish to express our appreciation of the liberal treatment and many courtesies extended to us by your company, which are the more noteworthy by reason of their occurring after we had accepted and paid for our apparatus. Having compared your light with nearly every other system, and having endeavored to familiarize ourselves with the subject of electric lighting in every possible way, we feel capable of judging, and warranted in saying that the Van Depoele Electric Light has no equal for brilliancy and steadiness. While the plants of other companies about us have met with "mishaps," our light has never failed us, and we find it indispensable.
Yours very truly,   SEA & CO.,
122 and 124 State Street.

OFFICE OF FOREST CITY ELECTRIC LIGHT AND POWER CO.,
ROCKFORD, ILL., August 2, 1883.

PRESIDENT VAN DEPOELE ELECTRIC LIGHT CO.:
Dear Sir,— Our plant of twenty lights here is running very nicely and giving entire satisfaction. I consider the Van Depoele light far superior in many respects to any other light I have ever seen, and shall take pleasure in recommending it whenever I get a chance.
Very truly yours,   GEO. L. WOODRUFF, Sec'y.

OFFICE OF TURNBULL WAGON CO.,
MANUFACTURERS OF FARM AND FREIGHT WAGONS, AGRICULTURAL WHEELS A SPECIALTY,
DEFIANCE, OHIO, February 17, 1862.
VAN DEPOELE ELECTRIC LIGHT CO., 203 and 205 VAN BUREN ST., CHICAGO:
Gentlemen,— Your favor of the 15th received. I am pleased to reply that the 16-light dynamo machine and lamps, set up in our wagon works, are entirely satisfactory, and you are at liberty to refer parties to us at any time. Very truly,
D. B. TURNBULL, Prest.

OFFICE OF NELSON KNITTING CO., MANUFACTURERS OF SEAMLESS HOSIERY,
ROCKFORD, ILL., July 1, 1882.
VAN DEPOELE ELECTRIC LIGHT CO., CHICAGO:
Gents,— Inclosed please find our draft in settlement for electric light apparatus as per our contract with you. We are pleased to say to you that, notwithstanding the difficulty of a low room and columns on the floor, to which our attention was called at time room was examined, the plant has given us entire satisfaction, and requires no more attention than can be given it by our superintendent, who has, besides, the care and supervision of eighty-five knitting machines.
Very respectfully,   NELSON KNITTING CO.

OFFICE OF CITY WATER WORKS, J. H. KERR, SUPERINTENDENT,
ROCK ISLAND, ILL., August 14, 1883.
PRESIDENT VAN DEPOELE ELECTRIC LIGHT CO.:
Dear Sir,— In reply to your communication asking if your light gave satisfaction, I would say that since I have been in charge of the water-works department (since June 1) the light has given entire satisfaction — could not be. better. Have nothing to do but keep the lamps clean, set the carbons and start the engine, and we throw the Brush light (that is in use in the city) in the shade.
In conclusion, would recommend the light to any one who contemplates using the electric light.
Yours respectfully,   JOSEPH H. KERR, Superintendent.

MILWAUKEE, WIS., August 14, 1883.
PRESIDENT VAN DEPOELE ELECTRIC LIGHT CO.:
Dear Sir,— We take pleasure in stating that the lights put up by your company in the National Park of Milwaukee are in every respect what you represented them to be. They burn very steadily and brightly, and are the admiration of all who see them. The work of construction of circuits, etc., is complete in every detail, everything being finished up in a workmanlike manner, and the apparatus put in absolutely perfect running order before it was left. We feel satisfied in recommending this light, and believe that it is superior to any other now in existence.
Respectfully,   BRAND & HUGHES.

OFFICE OF BURTIS BROTHERS,
IMPORTERS AND MANUFACTURERS OF FINE CIGARS, CENTRAL MUSIC HALL BUILDING,
CHICAGO, July 1, 1882.

VAN DEPOELE ELECTRIC LIGHT CO., CHICAGO:

Dear Sir,—Please send us some of your circulars descriptive of your system for electric lighting.

A large number of our customers and others, attracted by the unusual brilliancy of the light furnished us by your company, frequently ask for more detailed information than we are able to give them. But we are glad always to subscribe fully to the claims for superior strength and diffusive power made by you when the contract for the complete plant of electric light apparatus, covering dynamo-electric machine, nine electric lamps, and steam engine was awarded you.

BURTIS BROS.

YOUMANS BROS. & HODGINS,
MANF'RS AND DEALERS IN LUMBER, SASH, DOORS AND BLINDS,
WAUSAU, WIS., July 5, 1883.

VAN DEPOELE ELECTRIC LIGHT CO.:

Gentlemen,—Yours of the 2nd, acknowledging last remittance, received. Your electric light has been in use on our steamboat, " The City of Winona," long enough to have thoroughly tested its efficiency. It gives us pleasure to say it is satisfactory. Our pilots are greatly pleased with it. Perhaps other lights are just as good; we have had no experience with any other, but we would not care to exchange for any we have seen. Very truly yours,

YOUMANS BROS. & HODGINS.

DECORAH ELECTRIC LIGHT AND POWER CO., F. B. LANDERS, Secretary.
DECORAH, IOWA, August 10, 1883.

PRESIDENT VAN DEPOELE ELECTRIC LIGHT CO.:

Dear Sir,—Your plant purchased by us of thirty lights is in good condition. When properly run is the best light, we think, in use, giving a very steady light, and of much power, and would recommend it for extensive lighting purposes, such as general stores, factories, machine shops, hotels, street purposes, etc. Very truly yours,

F. B. LANDERS, Secretary D. E L. & P. Co.

ROCKFORD, ILL., August 17, 1882.

A. K. STILES, PRESIDENT VAN DEPOELE ELECTRIC LIGHT CO., CHICAGO:

Dear Sir,—This company, through its representative, spent considerable time in careful examination of the different systems of electric lighting, and notwithstanding the claims of other companies that the Van Depoele lights are not as represented, in view of the liberal guarantee made, it was decided to adopt your lights, which have been placed and are running to our entire satisfaction. One of our employes, with but one half day spent as an assistant for your representative to set up the plant, has shown himself fully competent to give the apparatus all the care required. ROCKFORD BOLT WORKS CO.

CHICAGO, October 3, 1883.

VAN DEPOELE ELECTRIC LIGHT CO., 203 VAN BUREN ST., CHICAGO:

Gentlemen,—At your request I have indicated the Porter-Allen engine which is now driving your lights at the Chicago Inter-State Exposition. The lights, as counted by myself, were ninety-two in number, and were noted to be brilliant, of a pure, white color, and very steady. The indicated power used for the above number of lights was on repeated trial found to be 77.9 *H. P.* After deducting ten per cent of this for the friction of the line shaft, engine and dynamos, we have 69.11 *H. P.*, or three-quarters of one horse-power per light as the amount of power actually used in the circuit. Very truly yours, N. C. BASSETT.

CHICAGO, October 5, 1883.

VAN DEPOELE ELECTRIC LIGHT CO., 303 VAN BUREN ST.:

I am now using your system of arc lights for photographic purposes at the International Exposition in this city, now in session, and am happy to say that my most sanguine expectations have been far exceeded, and my work is in every particular equal to results obtained by the sun, the likeness being very perfect and truthful. I have experimented with other systems of electric light, but never before even approached the standard of excellence obtained with the Van Depoele light. For this purpose the light must be absolutely steady, brilliant and diffusive, and the Van Depoele meets the requirements in every particular. Respectfully,

C. H. VAN DEUSEN, Photographer.

SUMMER GARDEN, CARL VONKUEHNAU, PROP'R.
CHICAGO, August 9. 1883.

PRESIDENT VAN DEPOELE ELECTRIC LIGHT CO.:
Dear Sir,— I have had my establishment lighted for the past two years with the Van Depoele system of electric lighting, and would not exchange it for anything else I know of. It is absolutely steady, and is the most brilliant electric light in the market, in my opinion.
Respectfully,   CR. VONKUEHNAU.

THE TOBEY FURNITURE CO., COR. STATE AND ADAMS STREETS,
CHICAGO, August 11, 1883.

PRESIDENT VAN DEPOELE ELECTRIC LIGHT CO.:
Dear Sir,— We have used a sixteen-light plant of the Van Depoele system of electric lighting in our store for nearly four months with satisfaction, pleasure and economy. The light is very steady and bright. We thoroughly canvassed the field of electric lighting and selected the Van Depoele light. You have the liberty of referring to us for reference.
Very truly,   THE TOBEY FURNITURE CO.

MILWAUKEE, WIS., August 15, 1883.

NORMAN T. GASSETTE, PRESIDENT VAN DEPOELE ELECTRIC LIGHT CO.:
Dear Sir,— We have now sixty lights of the Van Depoele system in the Milwaukee Exposition Building, which are giving perfect satisfaction, being in charge of our own engineer, and run at surprisingly small expense. The light given is steady and reliable, and for purity of color and brilliancy is equal to any we have seen.   Very truly yours,
R. P. JENNINGS, Secretary.

CITY OF ROCK ISLAND, CITY CLERK'S OFFICE,
ROCK ISLAND, ILL., May 9. 1883.

TO WHOM IT MAY CONCERN:
We, the undersigned, water works committee of the city of Rock Island, Ill., hereby express our satisfaction with the Van Depoele Electric Light plant as established here.
JAMES Z. MOTT. Mayor, Chairman Committee.
H. P. HULL.
WILLIAM GRAY.
Attest: ROBT. KOEHLER, City Clerk.

MOORHEAD, MINN., March 21, 1884.

VAN DEPOELE ELECTRIC LIGHT CO.:
We have used the Van Depoele system of arc electric lights, both for lighting of stores and streets in this city, for about twelve months, during which time they have given entire satisfaction. We have had no reason to regret our selection of lights, and should we at any time desire to increase the size of our plant, would add more Van Depoele lights in preference to any others. You have our consent to refer interested persons to us.
Respectfully,   MOORHEAD ELECTRIC LIGHT & POWER CO.
per EDW. E. MOORE, Secretary and Treasurer.

OFFICE OF CROOKSTON ELECTRIC LIGHT CO.
CROOKSTON, MINN., March 28, 1884.

VAN DEPOELE ELECTRIC LIGHT CO.:
The electric light plant bought of you we started up January 17, and up to date we have not had a single interruption of any kind. It gives entire satisfaction both to us and our customers. Those that were backward at first in giving orders for lights are now doing so after seeing its merits. We will soon be running to our full capacity. Would recommend the Van Depoele system to anyone contemplating buying a plant. Our plant was started up and has been run to date by ourselves, we having no previous experience in electric lights.
Yours respectfully,   JACOBUS & MATTHEWS.

BLOOMINGTON, ILL., April 3, 1884.

VAN DEPOELE ELECTRIC LIGHT CO.:
The forty-light Van Depoele Electric Light plant in this city is working admirably, we believe, and those who have had opportunity to compare our lights with those of other systems elsewhere say that we have as good lights as any in the country anywhere. We have in immediate prospect the increasing of our plant to sixty or one hundred more.
C. D. MEYERS, Secretary Bloomington E. L. & P. Co.

ELGIN, ILL., April 15, 1884.

VAN DEPOELE ELECTRIC LIGHT CO.:

We have used the Van Depoele system of electric lights since November last for the purpose of lighting the city of Elgin by means of the tower system, making use of six towers 125 feet high and one tower 150 feet high, placing thereon twenty-nine sixteen-hour-service Van Depoele Electric Lamps — four each on six of the towers and five on one of the towers. By this means we light the city in such manner that it has given perfect satisfaction to all citizens. Many of the most conservative and careful taxpaying citizens have spoken in the highest terms of the manner in which the city is lighted. The fact is that we light the city — not only the streets, but the grounds — the back yards and the door yards, adding greatly to the safety of persons and property. In our opinion no city can afford to allow its citizens to reside in darkness, when at a small expense they may secure a light that is a protection to persons and property — a civilizing influence of the first order.

ELGIN ELECTRIC LIGHT CO.,
by GEO. S. BOWEN, President.

WAUSAU, WIS., April 10, 1884.

VAN DEPOELE ELECTRIC LIGHT CO.:

It is now one year since we commenced using your electric lights in our mill, and, although handled by inexperienced men, we have not had the least difficulty in running it; nor have we had to put one dollar in repairs on it. The plant is as good as the day we bought it, and has given us the best of satisfaction. We think it better and cheaper than anything we have used or heard of. It has paid for itself and better in one year's work. We can do more and better work by it than any other artificial light we know anything about.

Yours truly, LEAHY & BEEBE.

CITY ENGINEER'S OFFICE,
WINONA, MINN., April 24, 1884.

VAN DEPOELE ELECTRIC LIGHT CO., CHICAGO, ILL.:

Gentlemen,— After a careful investigation the city decided upon and ordered electric-light apparatus of your system, which was started up about January 21. We put three lamps of six thousand candle power each upon our water tower, which work perfectly. We also put in twenty lamps of two thousand candle power, eight of them on sixty-feet poles, the balance suspended at the corners of the streets on a circuit of about two miles, and they worked beautifully, so well in fact that the people thought there were lamps enough to light the whole city, and as a consequence the lamps were distributed over the city on a circuit of ten miles, which was, in my opinion, a mistake, as the lights do not shine with that absolute steadiness as before the change, the dynamo being taxed a little more than it should be; but still the lights give good satisfaction and are hard to beat. Everybody who comes here from other electric-lighted cities say we have the best lights they have seen anywhere. The city has ordered thirty more lamps of your system and a dynamo to run them; when received we shall shorten the circuit run by the present dynamo to the length originally designed, when we shall have as good an artificial light as any on earth.

THOS. H. BOTHAM,
Engineer in charge Winona Water Works and Lighting Station.

P. S.— I am pleased that yours is a low-tension system, as in handling the dynamo while running I have received several shocks without injury. If this had been high tension, like some of your would-be rivals, my family would have needed the services of an undertaker.

T. H. B.

JOLIET, ILL., May 9, 1884.

VAN DEPOELE ELECTRIC LIGHT CO., CHICAGO, ILL.:

Gentlemen,— Replying to yours of recent date, relative to the use of the Van Depoele system of electric lighting by this company in this city, we are pleased to say that it is giving entire satisfaction, both to ourselves and our customers. We have sixty arc lights supplying the merchants. The Fuller company put a light in here, but our lights are so much brighter and steadier that everyone votes the Van Depoele to be the banner light, which is used exclusively, save a very few exceptions, but we will soon have them all. We send you a few recommendations from our subscribers.

CITIZENS' ELECTRIC LIGHT CO.

LLOYD EBERHART, Secretary.

We have in our store two of your lights and are highly pleased with them. They are entirely beyond our expectations, and can truly say they are the best electric lights we have seen, without any exceptions whatever. Respectfully,

JOLIET, ILL. BRAUN & RAUB.

We have been using your light about one month now to our entire satisfaction, and can say it is the best light that we have ever seen. Yours very truly,

JOLIET, ILL. WEBBER & WEBBER.

We have had your light in use now for nearly two months, and we are pleased to say with entire satisfaction. We unhesitatingly recommend it as the best light ever seen.

JOLIET, ILL.   Respectfully.   HARRIS & SAMTER.

We have been using the Van Depoele light in our store for about two months. We are well pleased with it. It lights us up in fine shape.

JOLIET, ILL.   WALLS & ADLER.

Have been using the Van Depoele light for sixty days and do not ask for anything better; perfectly satisfied.

JOLIET, ILL.   H. J. YOUNG.

MAYOR'S OFFICE,
WINONA, MINN., April 24, 1884.

A. K. STILES, ESQ., PRES. V. E. L. Co.:

Dear Sir.— Late last fall the city of Winona ordered of you three six-thousand-candle-power lamps, to put on the top of the water tower, over two hundred feet in height. They were started in January, and everybody is pleased. One of our citizens says that he can read fine newspaper print in his door-yard by the light three-quarters of a mile distant.

We also ordered at the time twenty two-thousand-candle-power lamps, which were distributed over the city. The citizens were somewhat dissatisfied because there was not enough of them. Trying to make everybody happy we have ordered thirty more, which we hope you will be able to start up the ensuing week. It is a beautiful white and clear light, and the best with which I am acquainted.   JOHN LUDWIG, Mayor of Winona.

OFFICE OF THE NOVELTY MANFG. Co.,
STERLING, ILL., May 13, 1884.

VAN DEPOELE ELECTRIC LIGHT CO., CHICAGO, ILL.:

Gentlemen.— Replying to your recent favor, our lights are running very good indeed. We have never had the least trouble with them since they started.— January 1st, 1884. Our generator is of thirty-light capacity. We run our machine half the night with five lamps, and during the evening we run twenty-two lamps. We are entirely satisfied with the economy and working of the apparatus, and believe we have the best artificial illuminant in the country. We would not go back to gas or gasoline at any price. You are at liberty to refer to us.

Respectfully.   NOVELTY MANUFACTURING CO.

OFFICE OF PEOPLE'S ELECTRIC LIGHT CO.,
STREATOR, ILL., May 14, 1884.

VAN DEPOELE E. L. Co.:

In answer to your favor asking how our light here is doing, I take pleasure in saying " it is doing well."

I have seen many electric lights in operation, but have never seen any superior to the Van Depoele, and in many respects I think there is no light equal to it.

It is unquestionably the most brilliant of the many electric lights now burning, and in this place at least we have no trouble with the "flickering" and "going out" which destroy the practical usefulness of some electric lights. Our people are satisfied with it, and we are constantly having calls for new lights. The fact that the people want it and pay for it cheerfully, after a competitive test with the Thompson-Houston light, convinces me that we have the best and most economic electric light in the country.   O. B. RYON.

Sec'y and Manager People's Electric Light Co., Streator, Ill.

ELGIN, ILL., May 14, 1884.

VAN DEPOELE ELECTRIC LIGHT CO., CHICAGO:

Sirs.— Since last November our little city has been basking in the bright illumination of the electric light produced by sixty of the Van Depoele lamps, furnished by a local company, Geo. S. Bowen, president. Twenty-nine of these lamps are on towers, and the balance in stores, offices, etc. I use one in my studio for photographic purposes, with excellent success, making negatives in from two to fifteen seconds. I may be considered a little egotistical when I say that I can, and have, produced as good pictures with one lamp of the Van Depoele system as some others who have used four or five of other systems, but such are the facts. The way we got the light was this : I was chairman of a committee appointed by the city council to select a light for lighting our city, and after thoroughly canvassing and examining the various electric lights we came to the unanimous conclusion that the Van Depoele was decidedly the best, and so reported. Our report was received and adopted and the lights ordered. We now claim too that we have the best lighted city in the world.   Yours.   G. H. SHERMAN.

DUBUQUE, IOWA, May 17, 1884.

VAN DEPOELE ELECTRIC LIGHT CO., CHICAGO, ILL.:

Gentlemen,—Replying to your inquiry regarding the working of your six-light plant in our saw-mill, we take great pleasure in stating that after having been put to the severest tests it has more than met our expectations in every particular.

We are running this plant with power communicated from our saw-mill engine, which, owing to the character of our work, is very variable. Notwithstanding the above facts, the light obtained is thoroughly satisfactory, and were the power such as to afford uniform speed, we believe it would equal, if not exceed, any arc light we have ever examined.

Very truly yours,   STANDARD LUMBER CO.

OFFICE OF COL. WOOD'S MUSEUM, CHICAGO, ILL., May 21st, 1884.

VAN DEPOELE ELECTRIC LIGHT CO., CHICAGO:

Gentlemen,— We are using your light in connection with our Museum, and are pleased to say that it meets our highest anticipation and gives the best of satisfaction.

Respectfully,   J. H. WOOD.

THE NATIONAL PANORAMA CO., CHICAGO, ILL., May 21st, 1884.

VAN DEPOELE ELECTRIC LIGHT CO., CHICAGO:

Gentlemen,— We have used the Van Depoele system of electric light for the purpose of exhibiting our Panorama of the "Battle of Gettysburg" for the past seven months, and cannot state but with pleasure that we are highly pleased with it.

Yours very respectfully, THE NATIONAL PANORAMA CO.,

EMILE GLAGAU, Manager.

LA PORTE, IND., May 22, 1884.

VAN DEPOELE ELECTRIC LIGHT CO., CHICAGO:

Gentlemen,— Since the introduction of the Van Depoele system of electric lighting in this city our merchants and citizens have been enthusiastic in their praises of the brilliancy and purity of the light. The lamps are distributed among the representative business houses of the city, and the light produced is considered the largest to be seen anywhere. We have thirty lamps in the circuit now, and it is believed that the city authorities will soon adopt this system for lighting the streets.

Respectfully,   C. H. MICHAEL,
JAMES O'BRIEN,
LORIG & WEBER.

OFFICE OF P. J. SAULSON & CO., LONDON TAILORS,
CHICAGO, May 22, 1884.

VAN DEPOELE ELECTRIC LIGHT CO., CHICAGO:

Gentlemen,— Our establishment is lighted with your system of electric lights, and we would cheerfully recommend it, and further say it is the most brilliant electric light in the market.

Respectfully,   P. J. SAULSON & CO.,
By C. D. HEWES, Manager.

OFFICE OF THE LANSING ELECTRIC LIGHT AND POWER CO.
LANSING, MICH., May 14, 1884.

MR. A. K. STILES, CHICAGO, ILL.:

Dear Sir,—The Van Depoele system of electric lights has been in operation in this city since December 17, 1883, and has proved itself to be the superior of all other systems. I have seen the various lights of other companies, as used in Chicago, Detroit, Cleveland, New York and Baltimore, and have no hesitation in stating that the electric light of Lansing is in my judgment the best I have ever seen. It has a peculiar brilliancy not possessed by the other lights, and yet it is not dazzling to the eyes, but on the contrary has something about it which makes me like to look at it. Customers all speak in flattering terms of it, and agree that it is the prince of electric lights.

Very truly yours,   E. C. CHAPIN, General Manager.

OFFICE OF BURLINGTON ELECTRIC LIGHT AND POWER CO.,
BURLINGTON, IOWA, May 22, 1884.

VAN DEPOELE ELECTRIC LIGHT CO., CHICAGO:

Gentlemen,— I take pleasure in assuring you that your electric-light dynamo for forty lamps, which was put in last February, has given us and our patrons entire satisfaction. We are running a very long circuit, having more than two and a half miles of wire, but find that the operation of our lamps compares favorably with those of any other system which we have seen, and we have examined the lights in various cities. In this statement I have the concurrence of every member of our board of directors. Very truly yours,

J. W. BURDETT, Secretary.

OFFICE SIOUX FALLS ELECTRIC LIGHT AND POWER CO.,
SIOUX FALLS, D. T., May 21, 1884.

VAN DEPOELE ELECTRIC LIGHT CO., CHICAGO:

Gentlemen.— Your arc light has been in operation here about three weeks, and we have pleasure in stating that up to the present it has given entire satisfaction.
Yours respectfully.
SIOUX FALLS ELECTRIC LIGHT AND POWER CO.
By THOS. RICHARDSON, President.

The Van Depoele Electric Light now in use in my store is one of the best lights I have ever seen. It burns without noise, don't flicker, and lights the store as bright as day.
BURLINGTON IOWA   C. K. WIGERT.

GREAT CHICAGO MUSEUM AND THEATER, W. C. COUP, GENERAL MANAGER.
CHICAGO, May 21, 1884.

VAN DEPOELE ELECTRIC LIGHT CO., CHICAGO:

Gentlemen.— We have been using your light in our museum and theater since we opened, and it has given us the best of satisfaction.   W. C. COUP.

JACKSONVILLE, ILL., May 19, 1884.

VAN DEPOELE ELECTRIC LIGHT CO., CHICAGO.

Gentlemen.— The forty-light plant of electric lights placed in this city by your company, are working to the entire satisfaction of everybody interested. We are running the full capacity of the generator, the subscribers pay promptly for their lights, and many of them say that they would not go back to gas no matter what the inducements might be. The light is steady and bright as a star. All that you have claimed for your light has been fully realized by us, and when the demand requires it we shall increase our plant with another Van Depoele dynamo.
Very respectfully.
JACKSONVILLE VAN DEPOELE ELECTRIC LIGHT CO.

MUSCATINE, IOWA, May 17, 1884.

VAN DEPOELE ELECTRIC LIGHT CO., CHICAGO

Gentlemen.— Replying to yours of the 12th inst. relative to the working of the thirty-five-light plant placed in this city by you, we are glad to be able to say that we are entirely satisfied with it. We think the light has a power of diffusing itself over a larger area than any other we have ever seen. The light is perfectly steady, and the patrons are well pleased with it.
Very respectfully.   MERCHANTS' ELECTRIC LIGHTING CO.

KANKAKEE PAPER CO., MANUFACTURERS OF STRAW BOARD, WATER STREET.
KANKAKEE, ILL., March 4, 1884.

VAN DEPOELE ELECTRIC LIGHT CO., CHICAGO, ILL

Gentlemen.— We have now had your system of electric light in our paper mill about six months, and we are pleased to be able to say *we like it.* It gives a first-class light, and in six months has saved us very nearly $500. We formerly used kerosene oil for lighting, afterward gas. We find the relative cost about the same for kerosene and electric light, and three times as much for gas.
Truly yours.   F. CRAWFORD, Treasurer.

LINCOLN, ILL., May 23, 1884.

VAN DEPOELE ELECTRIC LIGHT CO., CHICAGO, ILL.

Gentlemen.— Replying to your favor, it gives me great pleasure to state that the forty-light plant purchased of your company has to date given perfect satisfaction to consumers, and is doing all that you claim for it. I believe it to be as good as any light in the market, if not the best.
J. A. HUDSON.

OFFICE OF JACKSON ELECTRIC LIGHT & POWER CO.,
JACKSON, MICH., May 23, 1884.

VAN DEPOELE ELECTRIC LIGHT CO., CHICAGO, ILL.

Gentlemen.— Replying to yours of the 12th, say that myself, in company with two other members of our company, a few years ago, visited the East as a committee of our city council to investigate the different systems of electric lighting, and we carefully investigated the Edison, United States, Fuller and Brush; since then we have continued our investigations, and recently we learned of the Van Depoele, and now have one of your forty-light dynamos running, and propose to order another very soon. After carefully investigating the different systems, we concluded the Van Depoele the most perfect, and it has now been running nearly a month, and it gives the best and steadiest light of any I have seen, and our customers all seem to be well pleased with it.
Very respectfully.   W. B. REID, Sec'y.

FROM THE GREAT EXPOSITION OF JAPANESE ART.

ICHI BAN, SAN FRANCISCO. NEE BAN, CHICAGO.
WHOLESALE AND RETAIL.

COR. STATE & JACKSON STS., CHICAGO, June 3, 1884.
THE VAN DEPOELE ELECTRIC LIGHT CO., 203 VAN BUREN ST., CHICAGO:

Gentlemen,—TO WHOM IT MAY CONCERN. I have been a considerable user of the electric light for business purposes for the past three years, and in that time have used two makes other than the Van Depoele.

The thirty-light machine in use in Nee Ban gives better satisfaction by far than any I have ever used or seen in use, and I indorse it without any hesitation.

Sincerely yours, HORACE FLETCHER.

OFFICE OF GEO. D. FLETCHER,
MANUFACTURER OF SASH, DOORS, BLINDS AND MOLDINGS.
DIXON, ILL., May 30, 1884.

VAN DEPOELE ELECTRIC LIGHT CO., CHICAGO, ILL.:

Gentlemen,— I purchased of you in November, 1883, a six-light dynamo and lamps, and within four weeks had a twenty-light machine. I am running with water power, which I think has no equal for the business. My lights I have never found to be surpassed either for steadiness or brilliancy. They give me no trouble whatever, and I can say the same of the dynamo, as after starting I never go near it for any purpose whatever. When I started the twenty I filled the glass oilers and they are now about half empty, and good for six more months at least, without refilling. The brushes will last about six months and then they cost but a trifle to replace. The dynamo runs perfectly cool and steady, showing superior workmanship. My running expenses are $14 per month, which includes care of lamps. The dynamo and lamps can be handled with perfect impunity. I could not be induced to exchange for any other make. You are liberty to use my name for a reference at any time, and I would be pleased to correspond with any one contemplating the purchase of a plant. Yours truly,

GEO. D. FLETCHER.

H. F. NORRIS & CO., WHOLESALE JEWELERS, 29 WASHINGTON ST.
CHICAGO, August 7, 1883.

PRESIDENT VAN DEPOELE ELECTRIC LIGHT CO.:

Dear Sir,—We are lighting our establishment throughout with the Van Depoele system of electric lighting, and are entirely satisfied with it. Our clerks prefer the electric light to gas light. Respectfully, B. F. NORRIS & CO.

OFFICE OF MERCHANTS' ELECTRIC LIGHTING CO.,
MUSCATINE, IOWA, May 15, 1884.

VAN DEPOELE ELECTRIC LIGHT CO., CHICAGO:

Gentlemen,—In reply to your inquiry of yesterday's date, can say the lights are working charmingly. Our business has constantly increased almost every week since we started. We are running thirty-five lights to 12 o'clock each night, and are using about fifty cents' worth of fuel a night. We use a 50-inch by 12-foot tubular boiler, and a 9 x 12 engine, and one man takes care of the entire outfit easily. You are at liberty to refer to us at any time.

Yours truly, W. A. HARMON, Engineer.

TORONTO, ONT., May 24, 1884.

TO THE VAN DEPOELE ELECTRIC LIGHT CO., CHICAGO, ILL.:

Gentlemen,—For over four years I have made it a special object to investigate the electric light question, as I felt constantly inclined to engage in the business, and after lengthy examination of all the different systems now in vogue here and in the United States, I have come to the conclusion that your light is the only pure white light; that it illuminates more space than any light I have seen, and that in steadiness your light is far superior to any arc light in the market. This conclusion has led me to introduce your light in Toronto, and that in competition with another rival company; the result has again confirmed my views, as is attested by all those who compare both systems.

I think it only right and just to send you this for your benefit, for you really may boast to have the finest arc-light system now in existence.

R. G. LUNT,
Manager of the Canada Electric Light Co.

ECONOMY AND HEALTHFULNESS OF ELECTRIC LIGHTS.

(From Our Circular of 1880.)

These questions have been so thoroughly discussed through newspapers, magazines, pamphlets and manufacturing associations in Europe and America, and so well settled in favor of electric light that it seems but little more can be said, and a waste of time to reiterate what has already been stated.

The question generally asked is, How does it compare with, or what are its advantages over gas?

The electric light can be distributed through a given section from a central station by means of wire, which costs but little, to the place to be lighted, the distribution of gas requires large mains to be laid at great expense, below the reach of frost, and a large number of smaller pipes to be perfectly jointed at its thousands of crooks and angles. In mills and factories remote from the gas works the difference between the cost of mains and wires is no small item.

Gas light increases the temperature so as to greatly inconvenience the operatives in mills, clerks in stores and audiences in public places, while with the electric light the increase of temperature is scarcely perceptible. With gas light one is not able to distinguish colors; with electric light, tints are as easily distinguished as with sun light, of vast importance in manufacturing establishments, where colors are used, are obliged to have it for night work.

The electric light enables us to use and economize all space in stores, shops and mills; the articles or goods need not be arranged only in front of windows, but wherever the space is convenient, for this light is as pleasing to the eye and beneficial as day light.

Wherever large spaces are to be lighted, such as depots, mills, shops, streets, etc., the cheapness of electric arc lights in comparison with gas is much more fully demonstrated.

Further on we submit some statements from actual tests. It is safe to say that light with the Van Depoele system of arc lights is cheaper than gas at fifty cents per thousand.

With all other methods of artificial illumination, such as gas, kerosene, paraffine, naptha, etc., there is a large consumption of the oxygen of the air. Besides absorbing the life-sustaining properties of the air, burning gas gives out life-destroying gases. Each gas flame consuming five cubic feet of gas per hour produces more carbonic-acid gas in a given time than is evolved from the respiration of ten adult persons. Dr. William A. Hammond states: "A gas burner consuming four cubic feet per hour, produces more carbonic-acid gas in a given time than is evolved from the respiration of eight adult human beings." If the room or hall is not perfectly ventilated, it will therefore contain very impure air in a short time.

To perfectly ventilate, in cold weather, a store, shop or hall is an expensive undertaking; and as few owners of buildings are willing to incur the necessary expense, the occupants are compelled to breathe and re-breathe air poisoned by gas burned. When gas is burned in dwellings it has been found that the bindings of books are rapidly destroyed by the sulphuric acid produced, also, the walls and ceilings become dingy from smoke.

With the use of an electric light of 1,000 candle power, the oxygen in the air is not consumed to so great an extent as by one person; while were the same amount of light produced by gas, the oxygen used would be equal to that consumed by 1,200 persons, a figure which is appalling as we consider the effects of such an atmosphere. In a factory even considering a workman as a machine, it is economy to keep that machine in good condition, in order to obtain the best results. Mechanics already understand the whole matter, and prefer to work under the electric light, which keeps the head clear and body vigorous, to gas light which makes the head dull and body weakened.

In concluding this part of the subject we submit a few facts taken almost at random from a mass now before us.

A prominent manufacturer of this city among the Van Depoele lights, recently remarked: "Electric light is cheaper than daylight. I now use every part of my shop as a great saving and advantage, arranging machines in the most economical plan for the saving of labor, while before I introduced it I was compelled to locate that class of machinery requiring the best light near the windows, to my great detriment in loss of space on the works and time of the men."

From transactions of the New England Cotton Manufacturers' Association, by C. J. H. Woodbury, of Boston.

"It is convenient to compare the cost of electric lighting with the expense of gas in the same place; although it must be remembered that gas does not furnish as much or as good light, and is therefore not so valuable where quantity or quality of light is of importance.

In a weave-room, so very fine work, twenty-four arc lights replaced six sixteen-foot burners, which consume 393 x 64 1,753 feet per hour, so one arc light represents the consumption of (1,753 ÷ 24) seventy-three feet of gas per hour. A careful estimate shows there are lights to be costing 8.3 cents an hour; so this arc-lighting system represents one at eighty-nine cents per thousand. A similar estimate in another mill gives the annual cost of gas $2,189, and electricity at $1,125, or equal to gas at ninety cents a thousand. The annual saving to that mill in lighting expenses by the use of electricity makes a profit of $1,063, which represents six per cent on $17,716, without making mention of any improvement in work or production due to that light. In both of these establishments the lights were used about 450 hours per year. Other estimates give the cost of arc lighting equal to gas at from sixty-five cents upward per thousand. In the case of incandescent lighting, the cost is more difficult to estimate, because they are run at all degrees of brilliancy, affecting both the power and the life of the lamp.

The general opinion of a great number using electric light in a practical way is of more weight than the conclusions of any single investigator.

In the pursuance of my occupation as inspector, it has been my duty to examine nearly every textile mill and many other establishments in New England, New York, New Jersey and Pennsylvania, where electric lights are used.

I do not recall a single instance where the *quality* of the light was unsatisfactory."

From letters from mill proprietors read at the meeting:

" We have a thousand looms lighted with fifty lamps, giving ample light, more than we obtain with a gas jet at each loom. I believe that we could light more than twenty looms to a light; but with these we get a splendid light, which is the same to us as gas at sixty-five cents per thousand feet. We would not change back to gas."

Another:

" On account of the flood of light furnished the weavers, thus enabling them to make perfect work, as well as on account of the purity of the atmosphere, we feel that the production is increased to such an extent that we think that we cannot afford to do without it."

Another:

" Regarding the advantages of the light, it is better, safer and cheaper, and devoid of smell or heat."

Another:

" The excellence of this electric light consists in its brilliancy, steadiness, and freedom from tendency to vitiate the air. For our particular purpose it has also the advantage of being unaffected by the current of air from the dresser fans."

A cotton mill:

" Our experience leads us to the belief that a system of electricity is to be the artificial light of the future, especially in buildings of any magnitude."

Another cotton mill:

" We have always considered it a success as compared with gas, as being a better and more economical light."

A silk mill:

" We have twenty arc lights over seventy-five looms on silk and tapestry weaving. We consider the light far superior for our purpose to anything we have ever used. It is especially useful in distinguishing colors."

Cotton mill:

" Our help like the lights very much indeed, and are very anxious to get from the other mills into this mill, and assign as a reason the electric lights."

ELECTRIC LIGHT PORTRAITURE

ELECTRIC LIGHT PORTRAITURE.

ness, and the luminous rays thus divided, thus dispersed, fairly flood the person whose picture is to be taken. The clearness of the photographic image is superb. The face is softly lighted, and there is no hardness of contour — no deep shadows. The eyes of the sitter bear all the brilliancy of this light without any fatigue, without having to endure any disagreeable effects from the intensity of the arc. We give a detailed description of the reflector, because it is the one we adopted in our working by electric light at the late Chicago Exposition, with the exception that we put a Van Depoele lamp inside the reflector, which was allowed to run for several hours without any interruption whatever. We were enabled to have a light of the strength of from five to six thousand candle power. Mr. Van Depoele, the eminent electrician of the Van Depoele Electric Light Company, of Chicago, constructed a dynamo especially for our use, which gave an exceedingly pure white light of excellent quality for photographic purposes, which enabled us to make a negative in a few seconds.'

Yours respectfully,

C. GENTILE."

A Paper Read Before the Chicago Photographic Association. May 7, 1884.
by G. H. Sherman, Photographer, Elgin, Illinois.

(From Photography, May 15, 1884.)

"*Mr. President and Gentlemen,*—The subject before us to-night might well have been assigned to better hands, but I will do as well as I can to entertain you, and give you my method of using the electric light in photographic portraiture. I have had electric light on the brain, as it were, for a year or more, and having seen it established as a general illuminator in our little city of Elgin, I thought I would try it on negative making. I had talked with several who had used the light to some extent, and all thought it would do, but it was quite expensive, some parties having expended several thousand dollars in the experiment.

After witnessing the demonstration at Milwaukee last August, and having seen some of the work from other sources, I felt a little discouraged, but still I was bound to see what I could do with one light. I got no expensive plant — merely one light from a circuit of thirty lamps used in our stores. The lamp is of 2,000 candle power, of the Van Depoele system, for which I pay $12.50 per month. So you see that I hazarded very little in the trial. I have as yet attempted nothing but bust and half form, as my arrangement of the light is more adapted to these styles.

I will now give you a description of my mode of operating. We will begin with the light, which, as I said before, is one of the Van Depoele lamps, suspended near the center of my reception room. It is arranged with cord and pulley, so as to be raised and lowered to any elevation. I use a large, ground-glass globe. I wish to say in this connection that, as far as my experience and observation goes, I think the Van Depoele light is the best for photographic uses. We next have a circular concave reflecting screen of fine white muslin. This is also fixed to a standard, and made adjustable to any height and angle. This I place within a foot of my lamp. I also have a mirror about 16 x 24 made adjustable. Next are my screens, etc. On the side next my lamp I have a screen of white muslin, 7 x 8 feet. In the center and near the top is an open space 2 x 3 feet, which I fill with one or two thicknesses of blue gauze. This softens and diffuses the light. In the center of this gauze I place an oval piece of white tissue paper, sometimes two thicknesses, which I arrange so as to come directly between the sitter and the bright spark of the lamp. This also has a tendency to soften and diffuse the light. From the top of this side screen I have a projecting screen of the same material coming out over the sitter, adjustable to any angle. This, when used properly, serves to give the combined top and side-light effect. Next I have a large screen, or reflector, which I place on the opposite side of the sitter. This is also adjustable. I also have a hand screen or white muslin reflector which I use to throw the light in any direction and soften shadows. I use the ordinary background, or sometimes unbleached muslin. I light the whole or any part of the sitter or background with my mirror reflector.

This is my simple *modus operandi*, and if it will do anybody any good, he is welcome. I make no issue with Vanderweyde, Kurtz, or any of the 'high lights' in photography. I do not say that my way is best, or that it cannot be improved upon; but I do say that it is simple, cheap, and, with me, successful. I have received numerous letters from parties asking information, etc., all of which I have answered as best I could. I will say to any and all, Get a lamp and try for yourselves.

Have used the light for printing with good results; also in copying.

Hints,—If you use the electric light, *don't take tintypes.* Give full exposure, time about the same as with wet plate. Use the most rapid dry plates."

Note.—Mr. Sherman is having splendid success in taking electric-light photographs, as well as Dr. Truesdell, dentist, who uses one electric light in his office with excellent results.

PRESS COMMENTS.

Jackson, Michigan, *Citizen,* May 3, 1884:

The electric lights were set in operation for the first time in Jackson, last night, and it gave the city quite a metropolitan appearance. The light was a beautiful clear white color, presenting shades of brilliancy, but no flickering. All the hotels, and about forty stores have secured the light, and the first night's experiment convinces all that they will not regret it. Strangers from other cities say it is one of the best they have seen on their travels. The two lights on the tower at the works illuminate a large range of country, which before was in total darkness.

Bloomington, Ill., *Pantograph,* March 4, 1884:

The managers now decided upon purchasing a plant of their own, complete in every particular, and accordingly contracted with the Van Depoele Electric Light Company to supply an engine, boiler and complete outfit. The engine to be of 120 Horse-Power, guaranteed ample for one hundred and twenty-five lights. The dynamo and lamps used are the same that were utilized in lighting the Art Gallery in the Chicago Exposition last fall by the Van Depoele company, and which, by the way, took the first premium over all the electric lights there shown. The entire plant is in first-class running order and the patrons highly pleased with the light furnished. The company contemplates enlarging its business by adding another sixty-light circuit. The *Pantograph* congratulates the Bloomington Electric Light and Power Co., upon their success, and anticipates rapid extension of the Van Depoele Electric Light system in this country.

Winona, Minn., *Republican,* March 1, 1884:

At a meeting of the City Council held, July 31, 1883, a special committee was appointed to investigate the matter of lighting the streets and putting an electric light on the water tower. The committee submitted their report on October 1. They stated that they had visited Milwaukee, Chicago, Aurora and Madison, and examined thoroughly into the merits of electric light for public use. The lights examined were the Brush, Fuller, United States, Sperry, Van Depoele, American, Excelsior and Edison incandescent. The report of the committee was favorably received, and at a subsequent meeting the Van Depoele system was adopted. * * * Not only from among the citizens of Winona, but from hundreds of outsiders who have witnessed the operation of the Van Depoele Electric Light here, comes the verdict that as a brilliant illuminator and a steady light it is a fine success. Winona takes rank with the other enterprising cities of the Northwest in the adoption of this beautiful light.

Chicago *Tribune,* Sept., 1883:

One of the educational advantages of the present Exposition has been to demonstrate to the general public the extreme perfection and simplicity to which the science of electric lighting has been reduced. The most serviceable as well as the most valuable and attractive exhibit in the building is undoubtedly that of the Van Depoele Electric Light Company. Their 100 or more beautiful arc lights in the building are used not only in illuminating the booths of the principal exhibitors and the northeastern section of the building where their own stand is located, but also to light the art galleries and to take the place of the sun in lighting the photographic studios. The Van Depoele light was selected as being especially adapted for the art galleries, owing to its uniform steadiness, brilliancy, and purity of color. It has none of the injurious violet rays peculiar to some systems of electric lighting, the light being of a perfectly pure white color, while there is an absolute freedom from flickering. The Art Committee wanted a light that would be absolutely steady, brilliant and diffusive, and they selected the Van Depoele as being most suited for the purpose. A test by an outside expert was made during last week of the amount of power per light required, and repeated trial showed the amount used to be a little less than three-fourths of one horse-power per light. Electric lighting has now ceased to be experimentative, and the day when it shall supersede gas for all lighting purposes — even gas at fifty cents per thousand — is only a question of time.

Central Wisconsin, Wausau, Wis., June 2, 1883:

Monday evening, we were called to witness the lighting of the saw mill of Leahy & Beebe by electricity for the first time. The firm have purchased a five-light dynamo of the Van Depoele pattern, with an engine to run it. The lights are the same as exhibited here during the winter, and are said to be of the best pattern of arc lights. Five lamps are placed in different parts of the mill, and light up the whole structure as light as day. The first evening's experiment was quite successful. We have no doubt but that the example thus set will soon be followed by other mill owners. Thursday a large number of ladies and gentlemen, including the Common Council, visited the mill to see the light, and they all with one accord pronounce it a grand success. It excited the wonder and admiration of all beholders.

Muscatine, Iowa, *Tribune*, April 2, 1884:

* * * The guests at the opening were most highly pleased to see how successfully it operated. This lighting gave a favorable impression of what electricity would do. A little after 6 o'clock the engine was started up and in a few moments the lights were burning brightly. It wasn't quite dark when the lights were first turned on, but the store lights were brilliant, as were also the street lights. As it grew darker the lights grew more brilliant until it was a magnificent sight to look upon.

We were conversing with a traveling man at the depot last evening, and he was almost in ecstacy over the light. He said it was, without a doubt, the best light he had seen anywhere between Chicago and Kansas City, and he had seen a great many.

From the leading paper of the city of Elgin, where the Van Depoele light is in use to light the city:

The electric illumination of our city by the tower route is a success, as we had hoped it would be. It was a good success under the clear and tranquil sky of Saturday evening. It was a better success still in the clouds and storm of last night.

The satisfaction with the lighting is general, as was well exemplified at the Nolting House banquet that celebrated the successful outcome with a feast of reason and a flow of soul, etc. The banquet, by the way, was a bright affair, almost as bright as the illumination proper, and crowded full of sparkling wit, wholesome good cheer, and an unstinted measure of the good things of life. The assemblage was quite a representative one, and all in all a fair reflection of the brains and business of our bright little city.

Surely if the lamps hold out to burn as they started in, electric lighting will prove a large success indeed.

Extract from the proceedings of a meeting of citizens of Elgin:

Mr. Bowen's wish that the Elgin electric lights may always shed as beautiful effulgence as tonight was responded to by Frank Crosby, in the wittiest speech of the evening. There are disadvantages, he said, about this business, and he was a sufferer. His boy and he are in the Plymouth Rock business. After the electric light flashed over the city, he found a hen on the nest, thinking it was daytime and hence time to lay, It was all very well for his hearers to laugh, but what is going to become of his hens? To be sure, they would lay two eggs a day for a while, but then their constitution and by-laws would be ruined, and the traffic stopped. As a Plymouth Rock man he was opposed to the electric-light system. We must not take on too many airs and believe that as Rome had seven hills we must have just seven towers. If he has to sacrifice his Plymouth Rocks, he would as lief do it to eleven or nine towers as to seven.

Moorhead, Minn., *Daily News*, February 1, 1883:

Yesterday, in the evening of the last day of the first month of the year 1883, there occurred that which has commanded of late so great a degree of public attention, and the city, or at least the eastern portion of it, was brilliantly illuminated by that system which is to revolutionize all other methods of lighting. The people of the Key City have been looking long and anxiously for the coming of the electric light, and last night they had the pleasure of witnessing its inauguration.

* * * * *

At six o'clock last evening, the electrician who has the work in charge, standing by the electromagnet in the engine room of the company's works, closed the circuit. Instantly nine lamps at the Grand Pacific, the one at the corner of Front street and Broadway, one in Comstock & White's office, one in the store of G. A. Hendricks, one in S. H. Wright's furniture warehouse and one in John Mason's saloon, started out on their career of illumination, and straightway caused all other lamps that chanced to be burning anywhere near them at that time, to cast a shadow. At the Grand Pacific when the lamps burst into a blaze and filled the rooms with their bright, beautiful and steady light, all occupation was for a moment suspended, and everybody's eyes were fixed upon the objects from which was so suddenly transmitted a steady glare equal almost to that of the orb of day. In the billiard room were assembled a large crowd of men, who, after they had stood a moment in astonishment and surprise, commenced applauding heartily.

Everybody is pleased with the light, and it seems to meet the expectations of the most sanguine. Nobody cavils, but all unite in declaring the light which is evolved from between the two carbon points of the various lamps tried here last evening, to be purer, softer, steadier and more pleasing than any light they have seen elsewhere. One of the most pleasing features about this light, which in future is to make the streets of the Key City but little less light than day, is its color, or more properly speaking, its lack of color, it being a pure, mellow white, without even a trace of that violet or bluish tint which characterizes many, if not all, other electric lights.

www.ingramcontent.com/pod-product-compliance
Lightning Source LLC
Chambersburg PA
CBHW021555270326
41931CB00009B/1230